The
Saints
in
Mercy

The Saints in Mercy

PONTIFICAL COUNCIL FOR THE PROMOTION
OF THE NEW EVANGELIZATION

Jubilee of Mercy
2015-2016

Our Sunday Visitor Publishing Division
Our Sunday Visitor, Inc.
Huntington, Indiana 46750

Copyright © 2015 Pontifical Council for the Promotion of the New Evangelization Vatican City

Published 2015 by Our Sunday Visitor Publishing Division

20 19 18 17 16 15   1 2 3 4 5 6 7 8 9

Our Sunday Visitor Publishing Division, Our Sunday Visitor, Inc., 200 Noll Plaza, Huntington, IN 46750; 1-800-348-2440

ISBN: 978-1-61278-979-8 (Inventory No. T1739)
eISBN: 978-1-61278-987-3
LCCN: 2015946019

Translation: Bret Thoman
Cover design: Lindsey Riesen
Cover art: Shutterstock; Pontifical Council for Promotion of the New Evangelization
Interior design: Sherri Hoffman

PRINTED IN THE UNITED STATES OF AMERICA

TABLE OF CONTENTS

PREFACE

At the conclusion of the papal bull *Misericordiae Vultus*, Pope Francis wrote: "Our prayer also extends to the saints and blessed ones who made divine mercy their mission in life" (24). Among the pastoral tools of living out the Jubilee, a book dedicated to the saints had to be included. The title of this book, *The Saints in Mercy*, is significant. It expresses how the following individuals did not limit themselves to witnessing their faith through *works* of mercy; rather, they lived, first of all, *within* mercy, and as a result they expressed the beauty of it in the holiness of their lives.

We are particularly grateful to Father Antonio M. Sicari, O.C.D., for having given us the gift of this book, which depicts various "portraits" of holiness within which the face of mercy emerges. In just a few pages, he has represented the catholicity of the Church expressed by men and women from different parts of the world who have given voice to mercy. We will encounter several Italians, two Frenchmen, one Romanian, two Poles, and a Hungarian. We will meet a Chilean-Argentine, a Dutchman, a Belgian-Hawaiian, a Peruvian, and an Albanian-Indian. There are also two Americans, an Italian-Croatian, an Italian-Brazilian, and a Russian-German. The entire world and Church are truly represented. Not all are saints or blessed — some are still on the way to having their sanctity recognized by the Church. Nonetheless, they are all considered true saints due to their lively witness and profession of faith. As a great writer, Father Sicari has masterfully consolidated years of history. Here we refer to his writings on the topic of the saints which over the years have resulted in, to date, thirteen volumes collectively titled *Portraits of the Saints* (*Ritratti di Santi*). In them, readers will discover a profound treasure trove of saintliness.

As Pope Francis has said, the saints entered into the "depths of mercy." May your reading and meditation on their witness become a prayer of intercession to fully live out this Jubilee in unwavering certainty and confidence in the merciful love of the Father.

✠ Rino Fisichella
President, Pontifical Council for the
Promotion of the New Evangelization

INTRODUCTION

The title of this book, *Saints* in *Mercy*, was chosen over the more traditional expression "Saints *of* Mercy." It conjures up the many precious faces of Christians who throughout history have embodied Divine Mercy in the way they related with their brothers and sisters. They did so in such a "normative" and "exemplary" way that they have been officially recognized as models, patrons, and intercessors in the Church.

But if we reflect for a moment, we realize that they were merciful toward their neighbor because they first allowed themselves to become impregnated with the infinite Charity of God. They became *merciful* because they felt awash by *Divine Mercy*.

Like all believers, they, too, were initially confronted with the double commandment to "love the Lord your God with all your heart, and with all your soul, and with all your mind" and to "love your neighbor as yourself," which they sought to observe — not always successfully, we might add. But by persevering in humble obedience, they were eventually swept away by the "great love" (Eph 2:4) of the Triune God. Christian holiness, in fact, begins with the wonder we feel before the mystery of the Incarnation of the Son of God. Then we realize that he became both our God and our neighbor, having united within himself — once and for all — the two great commandments. And it is precisely this gift of being able to embrace both God and mankind — in one single Marian-maternal gesture — that brought Divine Mercy into this world.

Such wonder expands, then, to the point of longing when we

realize the extent which the Son of God strove to become our neighbor: he follows us inexorably along all our pathways and journeys; he takes our sins upon himself and forgives; he even anticipates and prevents us from stumbling. Thus, by living with Jesus (as Friend and Teacher; "the Way, the Truth, and the Life"; our Savior and Redeemer), it becomes possible for us to perfectly observe that ancient great commandment in the sense that it is he himself who works to impregnate all our heart, all our soul, and all our mind with love.

And, in the process, we become merciful, as good Samaritans who care for our brothers and sisters who have fallen by the wayside. This happens because we wish to *give back* to Jesus the gift of having become, for all of us, the original Good Samaritan. In this, we collaborate in his work of salvation. Once the Incarnation is understood in its merciful dynamism, it always humbly requests that we offer ourselves in the manner of Blessed Elizabeth of the Trinity who made the following well-known prayer in *Elevation to the Holy Trinity*: "Spirit of Love descend into my soul, and make all in me as an incarnation of the Word, that I may be to him a super-added humanity wherein he renews his Mystery."

The saints offer themselves, in fact, in many ways, so that charity becomes infinitely creative in them. It is, therefore, preferable to begin our hagiographic journey by speaking of "Saints *in* Mercy" as a reminder that everything is steeped in this mercy in each of their stories: their persons, their works and even the most painful vicissitudes of their lives. The mercy of God is, in fact, like a fire that burns and purifies everything it touches. And this Trinitarian fire has been burning since the beginning of creation. The important thing is not to seek to stubbornly escape it or keep oneself from his action.

CHAPTER ONE

The Joy of Announcing Mercy

St. Faustina Kowalska

St. John Paul II officially established the feast day of the Divine Mercy on April 30, 2000 — the same day as the canonization of St. Faustina Kowalska (1905-1938). For the occasion, the Holy Father said: "By this act I intend today to pass this message on to the new millennium. I pass it on to all people, so that they will learn to know ever better the true face of God and the true face of their brethren." Here the pope was evidently referring to the messages Jesus communicated to the humble Polish nun which she recorded in her diary (*Diary: Divine Mercy in My Soul*. Stockbridge, Massachusetts: Marians of Immaculate Conception, 1999).

There are primarily two riches conveyed to us:

1) The need for mercy

On almost every page of St. Faustina's long *Diary*, one perceives Jesus' yearning that his mercy may be known without any limit on it. Thus on April 4, 1937, Sister Faustina received this invitation from him: "Write this: Everything that exists is enclosed in the bowels of My mercy, more deeply than an infant in its mother's womb. How painfully distrust of My goodness wounds me! Sins of distrust wound Me most painfully" (*Diary*, 1076).

And on Christmas Eve of that year, she received the following message:

> In order that you may know at least some of My pain, imagine the most tender of mothers who has great love for her children, while those children spurn her love. Consider her pain. No one is in a position to console her. This is but a feeble image and likeness of My love. Write, speak of My mercy. Tell souls where they are to look for solace; that is, in the Tribunal of Mercy [the Sacrament of Reconciliation]. There the greatest miracles take place [and] are incessantly repeated. To avail oneself of this miracle, it is not necessary to go on a great pilgrimage or to carry out some external ceremony; it suffices to come with faith to the feet of My representative and to reveal to him one's misery, and the miracle of Divine Mercy will be fully demonstrated. Were a soul like a decaying corpse so that from a human standpoint, there would be [no hope] of restoration and everything would already be lost, it is not so with God. The miracle of Divine Mercy restores that soul in full. Oh, how miserable are those who do not take advantage of the miracle of God's mercy! You will call out in vain, but it will be too late. (*Diary*, 1447-48)

As one can see, words of boundless tenderness spring from the mouth of Jesus, and he welcomes and accepts everything. And yet, Jesus' words are definitively rooted in ecclesial language with references to the "tribunal of mercy" and the woeful warning to avoid falling into the abyss of "too late," which nevertheless remains a serious possibility if one so chooses. In a way as never before, the message given to St. Faustina throws open the depths of mercy, which can welcome and contain everything — except the derision of God.

In seeking to reconcile the justice of God with his mercy, Pope Benedict XVI's message to prisoners of the Rebibbia prison in Rome on December 2011 should never be forgotten:

> Justice and mercy, justice and charity on which the Church's charity is hinged, are two different realities only for the human person. For we distinguish carefully between a just act and an act of love. For us, "just" means "what is due to the other," while "merciful" is what is given out of kindness. One seems to exclude the other. Yet for God it is not like this: justice and charity coincide in him; there is no just action that is not also an act of mercy and pardon, and at the same time there is no merciful action that is not perfectly just.

And on the other hand, why would God continually offer so many heartfelt invitations throughout history to receive his mercy — embodied almost visibly in the words and gestures of his saints — if not for the clear urgency that it not be disregarded? The manner in which the saints invoke such mercy, proclaim it, and embody it is just as powerful as it is urgent — that is, the need to embrace it and risk the chance of despising it. The decision to no longer wish to remain in the lie is the only condition required to experience God's embrace.

2) Reflections of mercy

Not all the saints left us with reflections and insights about Divine Mercy. Yet they all showed us how to embody it in obedience to that Scripture which asks us to "be perfect, as your heavenly Father is perfect" (Mt 5:48), which we will see shortly as we examine their lives.

Regarding St. Faustina, instead of merely listing examples, let us seek to study and imitate the way she learned to pray, which was by imploring Jesus for the grace to become, herself, "*all mercy*":

I want to be completely transformed into Your mercy and to be Your living reflection, O Lord. May the greatest of all divine attributes, that of Your unfathomable mercy, pass through my heart and soul to my neighbor. Help me, O Lord, that my eyes may be merciful, so that I may never suspect or judge from appearances, but look for what is beautiful in my neighbors' souls and come to their rescue. Help me, that my ears may be merciful, so that I may give heed to my neighbors' needs and not be indifferent to their pains and moanings. Help me, O Lord, that my tongue may be merciful, so that I should never speak negatively of my neighbor, but have a word of comfort and forgiveness for all. Help me, O Lord, that my hands may be merciful and filled with good deeds, so that I may do only good to my neighbors and take upon myself the more difficult and toilsome tasks. Help me, that my feet may be merciful, so that I may hurry to assist my neighbor, overcoming my own fatigue and weariness. My true rest is in the service of my neighbor. Help me, O Lord, that my heart may be merciful so that I myself may feel all the sufferings of my neighbor. I will refuse my heart to no one. I will be sincere even with those who, I know, will abuse my kindness. And I will lock myself up in the most merciful Heart of Jesus. I will bear my own suffering in silence. May Your mercy, O Lord, rest upon me. (*Diary*, 163)

And Jesus observed her with pleasure and persistently confirmed, "My daughter, I desire that your heart be formed after the model of My merciful Heart. You must be completely imbued with My mercy" (167).

CHAPTER TWO

Gratitude for the "Just and Merciful" God

St. Thérèse of Lisieux

In our study of holiness, it might appear logical that those who have personally been down the long and difficult road of conversion or those especially devoted to works of charity would expound upon the theme of mercy. However, there is a saint who spoke of mercy in a particularly systematic way and whose life and message were dedicated to "spiritual childhood": St. Thérèse of the Child Jesus (1873-1897). She lived her own innocence as mercy to the point that at the end of her life she made an "Act of Oblation to Merciful Love of the Good God."

In fact, *Mercy* could have been the title for all three of the manuscripts that make up her autobiography, *The Story of a Soul*. She wrote the first of them (Ms A) — entirely dedicated to a candid telling of her childhood years — with one goal: "I shall begin to sing what I must sing eternally: 'The Mercies of the Lord'" (Ms A, 2r). She concludes, still singing with the Psalmist, "Give thanks to the Lord, for he is good, for his mercy endures forever" (Ps 136:1). But she is careful to clarify: "To me He has granted His *infinite Mercy*, and *through it* I contemplate and adore the other divine perfections!

All of these perfections appear to be resplendent *with love*; even His Justice (and perhaps this even more so than the others) seems to me clothed in *love*. What a sweet joy it is to think that God is *Just*, i.e., that He takes into account our weakness, that He is perfectly aware of our fragile nature. What should I fear then?" (Ms A, 83v-84r).

The second manuscript (Ms B) is a brief summary of her teaching in the form of a letter. In it, Thérèse simply comments on the biblical phrase, "For the lowliest man may be pardoned in mercy" (Wis 6:6), illustrated with the most beautiful image of the prophet Isaiah: "you shall nurse, carried in her arms, cradled upon her knees. *As a mother comforts her child, so I will comfort you*" (Is 66:12-13, NAB). And she turns to God with this surprising confession: "I feel that if You found a soul weaker and littler than mine, which is impossible, You would be pleased to grant it still greater favors, provided it abandoned itself with total confidence to Your Infinite Mercy" (Ms B, 5v). This is why she explained the following to a Carmelite sister in a letter: "What pleases Him is that He sees me, loving my littleness and my poverty, the blind hope that I have in His mercy" (Letter 197).

Her third manuscript (Ms C) concluded in the final verses with her song of the "mercies of the Lord." At that point in her life, Thérèse was able to testify that God was "surpassing all her expectations" from the moment she discovered in Scripture "a beautiful straight way, very short, a little and completely new way to go to Heaven: The elevator which must raise me to Heaven is Your arms, O Jesus" (Ms C, 3r).

Toward the end of her life, a missionary priest wrote to her confessing his spiritual anxieties regarding God's Judgment Day. Thérèse replied:

> I know one must be very pure to appear before the God of all Holiness, but I know, too, that the Lord is infinitely just; and it is this justice which frightens so many souls that is the object of my joy and confidence.... I

expect as much from God's justice as from His mercy. It is because He is just that He is compassionate and filled with gentleness, slow to punish, and abundant in mercy, for He knows our frailty, He remembers we are only dust. As a father has tenderness for his children, so the Lord has compassion on us (Ps 103:8,13-14).... This is, Brother, what I think of God's justice; my way is all confidence and love. I do not understand souls who fear a Friend so tender. (Letter 226)

In short, young Thérèse was able to unite within her heart the two characteristics of God that seem, to those of us who are too grown up, to be in contrast: mercy and justice. But this is because she put them both in direct contact not with the experience of human misery, which is manifested in sin, but with the even more radical experience of common creaturely poverty.

If God is moved by the presence of a sinner, it is because he is moved as by the presence of a child who has fallen (as a son or daughter who is hurt). Yet God is moved all the more because he created this young child of his out of nothing. Thus Thérèse abruptly reached the deeper insight at which theologians would arrive sooner or later: the act of creation is the first act of divine mercy; it established his future mercy for all people.

According to the young saint of Lisieux, God the Creator and Father sees before him only three kinds of people: the young child who fills him with tenderness; the young child who has fallen and is hurt; the young child whom he prevented from falling in the first place. At the same time God is infinitely just and merciful toward all three of these children who throw themselves into his arms, because "lowering oneself is precisely due to love ... and it is in bending down that the Good Lord shows his infinite greatness" (Ms A, 2v-3r).

Realizing that she had always been "prevented [from sinning]" by the Mercy of God and always "forgiven in advance," Thérèse invented for herself the following brilliant parable. [Presented are the same words in capital letters and italics as emphasized by her in the original text]:

> Let us suppose that the son of a skilled doctor encounters a stone in his path that makes him fall and that this fall causes him to break a limb. Immediately the father goes to him, lifts him up with love, cures his wounds, using for him all the resources of his art, and soon his son, completely healed, shows him his gratitude. Certainly, this child is quite right to love his father! But I will make another assumption. The father, having known that there was a stone on the road his son was traveling, hastens to go ahead of him and remove it (without being seen by anyone). Certainly, this son, the object of his provident tenderness, not KNOWING the misfortune from which he is freed by his father, would not manifest his gratitude and *love him less* than if he had been cured by him ... but if he comes to know the danger from which he has escaped, will he not *love him* even *more*? Well, I am that child who is the object of the providential love of a *Father* who did not send His Word to redeem the *just*, but *sinners*. He wants me to *love* Him because He *restored*, not much, but *everything* to me. He did not wait for me to *love* Him much as Saint Magdalene, but He wanted for me TO KNOW that I had been loved with a love of ineffable foresight, so now I love Him *madly*! (Ms A, 38v-39r)

Theresa's handwriting here reveals intense emotion while her words are at times so strong they seem to penetrate the sheet of paper: she is defending her discovery of love which she now attaches herself to with her entire being. She understood that the difference is not between those who have sinned and those who have not sinned; instead, it is between those who need love because they have sinned and those who needed *more love* to be able to avoid sin. And if the former love much because they know very well the "much" for which they were forgiven, the latter love only when they realize the preventive love they received. When they realize it — and this discovery of God's provident love is a great grace — then they are in the position of having to "love madly."

The possibilities, therefore, are not just two, but are actually three: there are those who love little because they believe they have been forgiven little; there are those who love much because they know they have been forgiven much; and there are those who love madly because they know that everything has been forgiven them in advance — they know, due to grace, they have not sinned! This latter category of people understands the Mercy of God infinitely more than those who have experienced it only in falling.

Whoever doubts the Little Flower should refer to that other great Doctor of the Church St. Augustine. Known for his troubled conversion, he expressed what she said in a similar way some fifteen centuries earlier:

> I will love you, O Lord, and thank you, and confess to your name, because you have put away from me such wicked and evil deeds. To your grace I attribute it, and to your mercy, that you have melted away my sin as if it were ice. To your grace also I attribute whatever evil I did not commit.... Yes, all the sins that I confess now to have been forgiven me, both those which I committed willfully and those which, by your providence, I did not commit.... Let him not despise me for I, who was sick, have been healed by the same doctor by whose aid it was that he did not fall sick, or rather was less sick than I. And for this let him love you just as much — indeed, all the more — since he sees me restored from such a great weakness of sin by the same Savior by whom he sees himself preserved from such a weakness. (*Confessions*, II, 7)

CHAPTER THREE

Ministers of Mercy

The Holy Curé of Ars / St. Leopold Mandic

1. *The Holy Curé of Ars* (St. John Vianney) (1786-1859)

Special reverence is due to all of those "men of mercy" who have been called to the ministry of the sacrament of God's mercy which they piously fulfilled. The Holy Curé of Ars (St. John Vianney) was convinced of this as he loved to say, "Priesthood is the love of the heart of Jesus." He also said, "A good shepherd, a pastor after God's heart, is the greatest treasure the good Lord can grant to a parish, and one of the most precious gifts of divine mercy."

He often used traditional and beautiful biblical images in his preaching in a particularly vivid and realistic manner. He once explained to his parishioners:

> Our Lord on the earth is like a mother carrying her baby in her arms. This child is badly behaved: he kicks his mother, bites her and scratches her. But the mother pays no mind. She knows that if she lets him go, the child will fall since he cannot walk alone. This is how Our Lord is: He bears all our ill-treatment; He bears all our arrogance; He forgives all our foolishness; He

has mercy on us despite ourselves. (Curato d'Ars. *Scritti scelti*. Rome: Città Nuova, 1976, p. 72)

At times, the holy Curé would encounter penitents who were discouraged and doubtful about God's forgiveness due to their awareness that they would sin again. St. John would then offer the following wonderful and inspiring response: "The good Lord knows everything. Even before you confess, He already knows that you will sin again and yet He forgives you. How great is the love of our God who even strives to voluntarily forget the future in order to forgive us" (Nodet. *Le curé d'Ars. Sa pensée - Son cœur*. Paris: Xavier Mappus, 1995).

And when his parishioners praised him for the deluge of sinners who flooded to their parish from all of France seeking forgiveness, he would humbly say: "It is not the sinner who returns to God begging forgiveness; rather, it is God himself who runs after sinners causing them to return to Him."

2. *Saint Leopold Mandic* (1866-1942)

Something similar took place in Italy in the first half of the twentieth century in the northern Italian city of Padua. Leopold Mandic, a Capuchin friar of Croatian origin, was constantly besieged by penitents who flocked to his confessional. (See P. E. Bernardi. *Leopoldo Mandic: Santo della riconciliazione*. Padua: Capuchins of Padua, 1983)

For roughly thirty years, he would spend between ten and fifteen hours a day in the privacy of his cell-like confessional listening to and forgiving sinners in the name of God. Due to his small stature and humble attitude, some people undervalued him, including his own Capuchin brothers. They said of him, "He was an ignorant confessor, too lenient, and he absolved everyone without discernment." Some even contemptuously called him: *Frate assolve-tutti* ("Brother absolves-everyone").

But he was sought after more than anyone else.

He always apologized humbly: "They say I'm too good. But if people come and kneel in front of me, is this not sufficient proof that they desire God's forgiveness?"

Another time he explained to some confreres: "You see, He himself gave us an example! We did not die for souls; instead, it was He who shed His divine blood. We must treat souls as He taught us by His example." He said on another occasion: "If the Crucifix were to scold me for being 'too lenient,' I would say in return: 'It was You who gave me this bad example, Lord! For I have yet to arrive at the madness of dying for souls.'"

And yet this friar who was so good and paternal had his own secret: the priest who welcomed everyone, reassured everyone, and offered everyone the certainty of the boundless Mercy of God, suffered personally from a constant and overwhelming fear of God's judgment. And he felt this even though he once humbly admitted that he had never committed a grave sin, saying, "I still feel I have the soul of a child."

Father Leopold was asked to live out and undergo the intense and painful beauty of this sacrament — even for his penitents.

In his later years, he was so distressed that he sometimes wept throughout the night while being assailed by an unknown terror. Like Jesus in the Garden of Gethsemane, he too sought out companions to stay with him. Even on his deathbed, witnesses said, "He looked like Jesus on the cross with the entire sin of the world weighing on him, and he felt abandoned by his heavenly Father." He had peace only while speaking to his confessor, when he received the same grace of forgiveness he so readily distributed to others.

Father Leopold did not suffer from any psychological disorders or senility. Instead, he had a very special calling from Jesus to participate intensely with him in his passion. While others had the luxury of spending their time discussing the issue of the indissoluble bond which much exist between God's Mercy and his Justice, Father Leopold had to actually live it together with Christ Crucified. In this way, he granted all mercy to sinners, while in his heart he took on all the rights of the Justice of God. In fact, he often said to penitents after forgiving them, "I will do penance for you!"

It is not easy to explain the glorious and challenging mission that God entrusted to St. Leopold — that of living out and experiencing (even for his penitents) the powerful and dolorous beauty of confession too often unheeded by so many Christians. Too many forget, in fact, that the Sacrament of Penance, together with the Eucharist, makes up the burning heart of Christianity.

We must constantly proclaim to every Christian: the mystery of the redemption is for you, for your own need for salvation, for your own destiny! And the Sacrament of Reconciliation is where you can personally participate in the Passion of Christ: first with the knowledge of having crucified the Lord of life (confession of sins), then with gratitude, thanksgiving, and adoration (forgiveness). And here is where the blood shed by Jesus on the cross descends directly on your soul.

CHAPTER FOUR

Mercy for the Least

St. Vincent de Paul / St. Damien de Veuster /
Blessed Teresa of Calcutta

The number of poor and suffering people is without a doubt immense. Yet among them are "the poorest of the poor." These live hidden where few dare descend, and, if possible, they would hide even from themselves.

1. *St. Vincent de Paul* (1581-1660)

In his native France, Vincent constantly sought out the poor in desperate situations, whom he believed the Lord had called him to care for personally. For this, he is known as "the saint of charity."

St. Vincent also opened up possibilities for women to enter monasteries of the world in an era when the cloister was the only option for religious life for women. Vincent outlined the new form of life for his Sisters of Charity in words that are now renowned due to the monumental changes they effected: "They will have no other monastery than the houses of the sick or the schoolrooms, no other cell than a hired room, no other chapel than the parish churches, no cloister but public streets or hospital rooms, no enclosure but obedience, no grate but the fear of God, no veil but that of holy modesty, for profession, constant confidence in Divine Providence and the offering of their entire being."

He gave the following instruction, shining like gold, to those sisters who took care of abandoned children (a real social scourge in his day): "You will be like the Virgin Mary, because you will be mothers and virgins at the same time. Will you see, my daughters, what God has done for you and for them? From eternity He established this time to inspire some women with the desire to take care of these little ones whom He considers his own: from eternity He chose you, my daughters, to serve them. What an honor this is for you!"

And since works and initiatives increased in Vincent's heart and mind — to the degree he encountered the needs of people on the street (the abandoned sick, elderly with no family, beggars, convicts, etc.) — he developed the habit of explaining to the sisters that each new work was precisely the way God rewarded the task previously assumed. And it was with this mindset that Vincent embraced and practiced all works of mercy, which were necessary to the society of his time.

When he decided to assume the care of those suffering from mental illness, he was ecstatic as he explained to his sisters: "Ah, my sisters, I tell you once again, there has never been a company [religious order] who should praise God more than ours! Is there perhaps one that takes care of poor insane people? No, there is none. And now this fortune is up to you! Oh, my daughters, how you should be grateful to God!"

Henri Bremond, the great historian of Christian spirituality, justly explained, according to St. John Paul II, "It was not love of men that led Vincent to holiness, but rather holiness that made him truly and effectively charitable; it was not the poor who gave him to God, but God, on the contrary, who gave him to the poor" (Homily, September 27, 1987).

True charity, in fact, derives from the gaze that never gets distracted, not even for a moment, from its focus on the living, familiar, beloved Jesus. Vincent himself always insisted: "The main purpose for which God has called us is to love our Lord Jesus Christ. If we depart even slightly from the thought that the poor are members of Jesus Christ, infallibly they will diminish the sweetness and charity within us." And his biographer recounted that the last word he uttered on his deathbed was "Jesus."

2. *St. Damien de Veuster* (1840-1889)

In 1865, a horrible leper colony was realized in Molokai, a rocky and barren promontory located in the Hawaiian Islands. As leprosy had no cure then, those inflicted with the illness were sent off to live there in total and perpetual isolation. Every month another ship disembarked with more sick people brought there by force. The island had telling names, such as "hell of the living" and even "graveyard of the living," demonstrating just how lawless of a land it was and devoid of all human solidarity.

It could have been said that mercy was no longer possible here. If the lepers' bodies were breaking down from complete lack of hygiene (they didn't even have fresh water!), their souls were breaking down in total depravity: sexual enslavement of women and children, all kinds of abuse, alcoholism and drugs, rampant theft, superstition and idolatrous practices — all were widespread.

And so it was for eight years, until the first white man voluntarily disembarked there on that island with a decision to live out a holy way of life in a hellish place: Father Damien de Veuster. He found himself among roughly eight hundred lepers who were considered "untouchables." A radical question was immediately posed to the new missionary: how to proclaim the merciful Incarnation of the Son of God. To do so credibly, the first form of evangelization would have to involve touching their diseased and corrupt bodies! "Evangelization" would involve difficult steps: placing the consecrated Host directly in their mouths, which were pink from their disease; anointing their hands and gangrenous feet with holy oil; tenderly bandaging their dreadful sores; allowing the children to throw themselves in his arms and caress him with their stumps; dipping his fingers, along with the hands of the lepers, during meals in the common dish of *poi* (meat mixed with flour derived from the taro plant); drinking from others' cups offered to him; and sharing his pipe with whomever asked.

Father Damien did not act in this way solely to respect the cultural sensibility of the Hawaiians — all the more acute for those who were sick; instead, he did so out of respect, so to speak, for "the sensibility of the Church," which is by definition "the Body of Christ." All sacraments and works of the Church are signs of a "physical contact" — salvific — between the humanity of Christ and our own suffering humanity. If desired "contact" was a sensitive and important cultural issue for the Hawaiians, for Father Damien it was also a question of faith.

Known as the "apostle of the lepers," Father Damien performed countless works of mercy. But if one had to choose and describe his most significant and effective work, we should remember one that was usually not very frequently or urgently practiced by Christians. The catechism formulates it in this way: "bury the dead."

It was the most humane thing he could have done in Molokai given that cures for leprosy were ineffective and even pointless. Instead, only one thing was certain: death. Thus Father Damien decided to reverse the usual order used in education: if for other Christians it was important to learn how "to live well in order to die well," for the lepers of Molokai it was necessary "to learn how to die well in order to live well." If we consider that, before his arrival, corpses were abandoned in the open air and even fed to the pigs, we can understand the impact of the missionary's decision to "celebrate death" and give it full human dignity. In that era, lepers were known as "the living dead" and the government was even about to pass a law to declare them "legally dead." Therefore, death — in all its associated ugliness and depravity — permeated the island.

With holy intelligence, Father Damien realized that he had to start by making death sacred and instilling it with Christian faith in the Resurrection. Therefore, he built a beautiful cemetery next to his hut. He also founded a confraternity of funerals. He tasked its members with the construction of wooden coffins and the accompaniment of the deceased to their final resting place with prayer, music, and the beating of drums. This ceremony occurred at least three times a week: it called everyone to silence and prayer, which replaced the anger and drunkenness they were accustomed to.

Later on, it was easier to organize the islanders in various other confraternities to provide for the people's most important needs: there was one for the care of abandoned children; another for the education of girls; one that provided visits to the sick; another for the construction of churches and housing; and one for the maintenance of the huts. The various "confraternities" became de facto structures of civic life and social assistance that no one could have ever imagined. Depending on the occasion, Father Damien himself played the role of planner, architect, digger, bricklayer, and carpenter. And he eventually undertook the construction of small schools, dispensaries, health clinics, aqueducts, and water reservoirs.

Due to a profound mindset, which only a saint can immediately grasp, his second great work of mercy was the implementation of the solemn celebration of the feast of Corpus Christi. This became the most beautiful and moving feast on the island as it was celebrated with musical performances of exceptional beauty.

He was also able to introduce the devotion of Perpetual Adoration. It was not easy for the sick people to observe the various shifts and changing hours, day and night. Yet, when "worshipers" were not able to enter the church, they could still kneel in prayer from their beds.

Father Damien himself was eventually stricken with leprosy. And when he saw that his body was beginning to break down (though he was not yet fifty years old), he humbly wrote to his superiors: "I have become a leper. I think it will not be long before I am disfigured. Having no doubt about the true nature of my illness, I remain calm, resigned, and quite happy in the midst of my people. The Good Lord knows well what is best for my sanctification, and I constantly say with all my heart: Thy will be done."

Since then, whenever he used the expression "my sick members," it appeared he was speaking simultaneously of his own suffering limbs, as well as the sick in his community, which he considered in a Christian way to be "like the Body of Christ and his own body."

3. *Blessed Teresa of Calcutta* (1910-1997)

Blessed Mother Teresa of Calcutta also dedicated herself to the connection between worship of the Eucharist and works of mercy.

She began her difficult mission with the following prayer, which was already a plan in and of itself:

> My God ... I do not want to go back. The poor are my community. Their security is mine. Their health is my health. My roof is that of the poor. Not simply those who are poor, but the poorest of the poor: those whom others will not approach for fear of being infected, of getting dirty; those who do not go to church because they have no clothes to wear; those who do not eat because they have no more strength; those who collapse in the streets knowing they are about to die while the living pass by ignoring them; those who are no longer able to cry because they have no more tears.

But where did she find the secret and strength to truly embrace every marginalized person with such sweet charity? She later explained the answer to her sisters: "Did you see how the priest treats the body of Christ with such love and gentleness during the Holy Mass? Try to do the same in the houses [of the dying] you visit: there you will discover Jesus in the guise of pain."

And many of her sisters later said that they completely understood that Eucharistic expression "the Real Presence of Jesus" when touching the aching limbs of the sick. And Mother Teresa explained the true identity of her institute of charity precisely in virtue of the sublime "Eucharistic identification":

> Above all, we are religious sisters. We are not social workers, teachers, nurses or doctors.... The difference between us and social workers is this: they do it for something, but we do it for Someone. We serve Jesus in the poor, and we do all this for Him. Everything we do — prayer, work, sacrifices — we do for Jesus. Our life does not have any other meaning, any motivation other than Him who loves us deeply. Jesus is the only meaning of our life.

And her sisters still take care of the "poorest of the poor" even today: unborn children, deformed children, abandoned children, single mothers rejected by their family, lepers, prostitutes, prisoners, the homeless, alcoholics, the severely handicapped, the mentally ill, victims of wars, drug addicts, AIDS patients, and the dying.

To those who asked her for more detailed information on her program and how she intended to organize her "works of mercy," Mother Teresa replied that she always strove to have the same beginning, the same middle, and the same end. She explained it this way:

- The beginning: "We always start by cleaning latrines: this is how we begin to open hearts."
- The middle: "I love Jesus with all my heart and with all my being. I gave him everything, even my sins, and He has surrounded me in the tenderness of His love. Now and forever I belong completely to my Crucified Spouse."
- The end: "Working for the sanctification of the poor, to give saints to God."

And it certainly is impressive to have a saint who understands how works of mercy indicate a navigable and straight road from the most humble places on the planet all the way to the most glorious seats in heaven.

CHAPTER FIVE

Recognizing the Suffering Face of Christ

St. John of God / St. Camillus de Lellis / St. Joseph Benedict Cottolengo

1. *St. John of God* (1495-1550)

John is considered "the creator of the modern hospital." Yet he did not limit himself to caring for the sick; the care he offered included all the works of mercy. He wrote in a letter:

> So many poor people come here that I very often wonder how we can care for them all, but Jesus Christ provides all things and nourishes everyone. Many of them come to the house of God, because the city of Granada is large and very cold, especially now in winter. More than a hundred and ten are now living here, sick and healthy, servants and pilgrims. Since this house is open to everyone, it receives the sick of every type and condition: the crippled, the disabled, lepers, mutes, the insane, paralytics, those suffering from scurvy and those bearing the afflictions of old age, many children, and above all countless pilgrims and travelers, who come here, and for whom we furnish the fire, water, and salt, as well as the

utensils to cook their food. And for all of this no payment is requested, yet Christ provides. I work here on
borrowed money, a prisoner for the sake of Jesus Christ.

He had a remarkable way of receiving and treating the mentally ill. Pietro Bargellini [a seventeenth-century bishop] wrote of
him: "Even if John never had any formal medical studies, he proved
better than many doctors." Of particular note was his approach
to treating mental illness. With great foresight, he introduced the
psychoanalytic method which Freud and his disciples would boast
of some four centuries later.

To this day, the name of the institute he founded, *Fatebene-
fratelli*, is still particularly significant [in Italian, the expression
means, "Do Good Brothers"; in English, the name of the congregation is the Brothers Hospitallers of St. John of God]. The term
dates back to the way St. John of God used to beg alms for his
patients: "Do you want to do good to yourself? My brothers, for
the love of God, do good to yourselves!" In fact, people cannot truly
love the poverty within others unless they first discover their own
pain within. This is the origin of the saying, "Do good to oneself
by doing good to others."

2. *St. Camillus de Lellis* (1550-1614)

We can have the same face of mercy as that of Christ who
embodied the way the Father looks at every person. However, it
will depend on whether or not we first contemplate Jesus. This,
then, will drive us toward identification. This is how St. Camillus
de Lellis acted. He not only demanded the best for his patients — to
the point of wanting to manage the entire hospital himself — but
he first demanded "tenderness" of himself and of his collaborators.

Camillus would personally receive and embrace patients as they
entered through the door of the hospital: he washed and kissed their
feet; he removed their rags and dressed them in clean gowns; and
he placed them in a freshly made bed. He wanted people to help

him "not for reward, but voluntarily so they would serve the sick for the love of God with the same tenderness as mothers treat their own sick children."

His assistants learned from him: "When he held sick people in his arms to change their sheets, he did so with so much love and care that he appeared to be handling Jesus Christ himself." At times he exhorted his assistants: "More heart! I want to see more maternal affection!" Or: "Use your hands with more soul!" Camillus was not afraid to use his bare hands to clean the faces of sick people disfigured by tumors that he then kissed. He would explain to all those present how "poor sick people are the heart and the apple of the eye of God, and therefore what we do to the poor we do to God himself."

For him, patients were a prolongation of the suffering humanity of Christ. He demonstrated this attitude on certain occasions without even realizing it. One biographer wrote:

> One night they saw him kneeling before a poor sick man who had such a disgusting and foul tumor in his mouth that the stench was unbearable. And despite all that, Camillus spoke to him very closely, almost "mouth to mouth," whispering words of great affection. He seemed wild with love as he referred to him with peculiar expressions: "My Lord, my soul, what can I do to serve you?" It was as if he thought this man was his beloved Lord Jesus Christ.

Another witness even said: "On several occasions I saw him crying vehemently and moved at the thought that Christ was in the poor man. For this reason, he loved the sick person as the person of the Lord."

His expressions may seem somewhat exaggerated to us. But certainly the impression of those who knew Camillus was not overstated. For in him there was no separation between active mercy toward his neighbor in need and tenderness for the person of Christ himself. In fact, they were so united that he once wept while recounting the sins of his past life to a poor person with the conviction that he was speaking to Jesus. In his eyes and in his heart Jesus was never an *ideal*, a *value*, a *cause*, or a *course of action*. Instead, he was and remained a loving and adored Presence.

3. *St. Joseph Benedict Cottolengo* (1786-1842)

He is universally known for having built the Little House of Divine Providence in Turin, Northern Italy. Its mission was to always have "providence as its foundation, charity of Christ as its soul, prayer as its support, and the poor at its center." The main feature of the house consisted in offering shelter to anyone who had none — especially the terminally ill and those with the worst diseases. It was run with the criterion of offering a proper "family" to every sort of people in need. It was made up of the residents, their assistants, volunteers, and all the staff necessary for their care to the point of becoming practically a series of veritable small towns.

In fact, the communities were built gradually, and were based on the different needs of the people who arrived at the door: there was a building intended for the mentally ill (whom St. Joseph Cottolengo referred to as "my dear friends") and another one for the deaf; there was an area for the disabled and another for orphans; there was a house for the terminally ill, and so on. The saint gave expressive Christian names to each building: "House of Faith," "House of Hope," "House of Our Lady," and "Bethlehem." He affectionately referred to the development in its entirety as "My Noah's Ark." Many were struck by his brilliant creativity, and some suggested a new name, "University of Christian Charity."

Cottolengo passionately taught his collaborators, saying:

> The poor are Jesus — they are not an image of him. They are Jesus in person. As such, you must serve them. All the poor are our masters, but those who are so repulsive

with the naked eye are actually our highest masters —
our true jewels. If we do not treat them well, they will
kick us out of the Little House. They are Jesus.

Therefore, he demanded that all exercise charity "with
enthusiasm and with joy."

CHAPTER SIX

Mercy for the Little Ones

St. Jerome Emiliani / St. John Bosco

1. *St. Jerome Emiliani* (1481-1537)

St. Jerome Emiliani is not very well known. All the same, the Church has given him a special title: "Universal Patron Saint of Orphans and Abandoned Youth." He was a nobleman in Venice at a time when his native city and the whole of Europe were devastated by famine and the plague. Rather than seeking refuge behind his nobility and comfortable social status, Jerome instead listened to "the infinite lament of the poor" where he discovered the gift of the "sweet occasion" of God to finally give all he had to his beloved crucified Jesus.

Over the course of a few days, he sold all his tapestries, rugs, and silverware. By day, he spent the money he earned to assist as many poor people as possible, while at night he went through the city gathering up the sick and burying the corpses he found abandoned in the Venetian alleyways.

Eventually, he gathered around him several hundred homeless children, creating a type of extended family for them. He provided the youngsters with vocational teachers in addition to the means and classrooms to educate them. In this, he introduced them to a dignified life of work. Thus he created a school of arts and crafts utilizing the educational method known as "participation and shared responsibility." The pillars of the school were prayer, charity, and work.

He was known affectionately by his friends as "the vagabond of God" and "the pilgrim of charity." Though a layperson, Jerome also welcomed priests as coworkers over the years who regarded him as a father, teacher, and spiritual guide. Eventually, he founded a religious order known as the Company of the Servants of the Poor.

2. *St. John Bosco* (1815-1888)

St. John Bosco deserves to be remembered in a special way as this Jubilee Year of Mercy corresponds to the bicentenary of his birth. The entire Church recognizes him as a true genius of education that he based on the "preventive system" aimed directly at the child's heart. He was particularly noted for the gift of being able to combine the severity of reprimand and discipline with the sweetness of a smile. Those who observed him during those moments said: "In the saints — as in God — justice and mercy kiss ineffably." When Don Bosco, as he was known popularly, spoke to his young people about the confession, he did so in order to help them understand that "hope, mercy, and confession were synonymous" for him.

It is estimated that Don Bosco assisted and educated over one hundred thousand troubled youth in his oratories. He labored tremendously for them: he devised the first "work schools," signing the apprenticeship contracts himself; he created the first night and weekend schools; he initiated the first mutual aid societies for workers; and he developed the first "Italian Youth Library," personally editing 204 small volumes. He even had his own special gallery at the Italian Fair of Industries and Arts held in Turin in 1884, an international exhibition.

Everything Don Bosco did for his boys sprang from an inner oath he once made to God. He explained to his boys: "I promised

God that until my last breath I will have lived for my poor young people. I study for you. I work for you; I am also ready to give my life for you. Take note that whatever I am, I have been so entirely for you, day and night, morning and evening, at every moment."

CHAPTER SEVEN

Wealth at the Service of Poverty

St. Elizabeth of Hungary /
Servant of God Friedrich Joseph Haass /
Blessed Vladimir Ghika

1. *St. Elizabeth of Hungary* (1207-1231)

Despite the fact she was a queen, St. Elizabeth fell in love with the ideals preached by Francis of Assisi who was then still alive. And, in fact, there were many royal princesses at that time who dreamed of imitating Clare of Assisi — at least as tertiaries. Those who, for one reason or another, could not leave their luxurious castles to live in poverty chose instead to "live within the splendid walls of charity."

Elizabeth began by building a hospital near her castle to deal with the scourge of a terrible famine that had struck her land. All who were not able to take care of themselves were ordered to be accepted and admitted: the sick, the hungry, and beggars of all sorts began pouring in. The queen reportedly "went so far as to distribute toward charity the proceeds of her husband's four principalities and even to sell her own costly clothes and items of value."

When her husband died, Elizabeth left her well-to-do relatives in order to live in a new hospital she had built where she could serve the sick personally. Her confessor guided her attentively and monitored her so that she would not become excessive. Yet every now and then, he realized that Elizabeth kept certain poor people hidden close to her. There was a paralytic boy, for example, who suffered from frequent bowel leakage whom she kept in her own chamber; there she personally kept watch over him and assisted him night after night. There was also a little girl with leprosy whom she personally cared for as if the girl were her own daughter. There was another child covered with scabies whom also she served humbly.

At the young age of twenty-four, Elizabeth died, "worn by compassion." Though her life was short, she spent all of it to reclaim the sublime Christian dignity for all the poor of her kingdom. She was canonized just four years after her death and subsequently proclaimed Patroness of Catholic Charities, as well as the patron saint of widows, orphans, the sick, beggars, the unjustly persecuted, and all the suffering. But it is not surprising that some prefer to simply call her instead the "Saint of Justice."

2. Servant of God Friedrich Joseph Haass (1780-1853)

Of German origin, Friedrich Joseph Haass was invited to practice his medical profession in Russia where he became the head physician of the Moscow prison hospital system. He carried out his mission with true and total mercy for the prisoners. The famous Russian writer Fyodor Dostoyevsky knew him personally and described him in his novel *The Idiot*:

> In Moscow, there was an old state counsellor, a civil general, who, all his life, had been in the habit of visiting the prisons and speaking to criminals. Every party of convicts on its way to Siberia knew beforehand that on the Vorobeef Hills the "old general" would pay them a visit. He did all he undertook seriously and devotedly. He would walk down the rows of the unfortunate prisoners, stop before each individual and ask after his needs — he never sermonized them; he spoke kindly to them — he

gave them money; he brought them all sorts of necessaries for the journey, and gave them devotional books, choosing those who could read, under the firm conviction that they would read to those who could not, as they went along. He scarcely ever talked about the particular crimes of any of them, but listened if any volunteered information on that point. All the convicts were equal for him, and he made no distinction. He spoke to all as to brothers, and every one of them looked upon him as a father. When he observed among the exiles some poor woman with a child, he would always come forward and caress the little one, and make it laugh. He continued these acts of mercy up to his very death; and by that time all the criminals, all over Russia and Siberia, knew him!

Another writer, Maxim Gorky, also spoke of him, calling him "the humanist of action." He compared him to St. Francis, recognizing that both possessed "the overall happiness of love."

A particular quality of Haass was that he gathered around him numerous collaborators who dedicated themselves to cultivating within the prisons the "beauty of mercy" — an ideal highly esteemed by the Russian people.

When he died, the countless poor he had assisted blessed him. While Haass lying on his deathbed, the holy patriarch of Moscow, Philaret himself, arrived and offered the following words of comfort: "Your life is truly full of grace. Full of grace are your works. In you the words of the Savior are fulfilled: 'Blessed are the meek; Blessed are those who hunger and thirst for righteousness; Blessed are the merciful; Blessed are the pure in heart; Blessed are the peacemakers ...' [cf. Matthew 5:5-10]. My brother, yours is the kingdom of heaven."

3. *Blessed Vladimir Ghika* (1873-1954)

Another blessed who deserves to be remembered for mercy (as well as for his profundity of thought) is Vladimir Ghika. Not very well known, but particularly expressive of mercy, this Romanian prince converted to Catholicism. He was also a martyr, as declared by Pope Francis in 2013.

At the beginning of the tormented twentieth century, he was ordained a priest in Romania where, inspired by St. Vincent de Paul, he founded the first Catholic organization dedicated to works of charity. There had never been such an institute there. He threw himself into his work and spent all his energy and possessions on the poor and the sick.

In the process, he elaborated on what he referred to as "liturgy of our neighbor," which was constantly in his thoughts and in the formation he passed along to his followers. He wrote a book in French with the significant title *La liturgie du Prochain* (in English: *The Liturgy of Our Neighbor*) [V. Ghika, *Entretiens Spirituels. La Liturgie du prochain*. Paris: Beauchesne, 1997], meaning that we must celebrate "the encounter of Jesus with Jesus" while visiting the poor.

He wrote:

> It is a double and mysterious liturgy when the poor person sees Christ come to him in the guise of the one who befriends him. And the benefactor sees before him the suffering Christ who appears in the poor and leans on him. But, for that very reason, it is one liturgy. In fact, if the gesture is effected as it should be, there is only Christ on both sides: Christ the Savior comes to the Suffering Christ, and both are integrated in the glorious and blessing Risen Christ.

Thus the Eucharistic liturgy — already celebrated on the altar — is extended in the visit to the poor. It is nothing other than "enlarging the Mass in the day and in the entire world, like concentric waves that propagate beginning from the Eucharistic communion of the morning."

For this reason, when Vladimir was called on to serve, he set out praying:

> Lord, I am going to another one of those whom you have called "another yourself." May the offering I am about to bring and my heart with which I give it be well received by my suffering brother or sister. May the time I spend with them bear fruit of eternal life — for them and for me. Lord, bless me with the hand of your poor. Lord, sustain me with the gaze of your poor. Lord, receive me, too, one day in the holy company of your poor.

His favorite saying was: "Nothing renders God as close as one's neighbor." He definitely put this into practice in the final months of his life when he was thrown into a horrendous Communist prison at the age of eighty. Despite the dreadful conditions, he encouraged the other prisoners affectionately and attentively by telling stories as if an elderly grandfather. Commenting on the Gospel passage of the appearance of Jesus to the disciples on the Road to Emmaus (cf. Luke 24:13-35), he said to them: "When the day ends, the disciples of Jesus can be recognized only by the way they, like their master, know how to 'break bread' by sacrificing the living bread of their own bodies for their brothers."

CHAPTER EIGHT

Mercy for the Marginalized

St. Martin de Porres / St. Katharine Mary Drexel /
Servant of God Dorothy Day /
Servant of God Brother Ettore Boschini

1. *St. Martin de Porres* (1579-1639)

Martin was the illegitimate son of a nobleman and a slave woman. As such, in the era and society in which he lived then in Peru, he merited only the derogatory title of "mulatto dog." But in the end, due to the dedication with which he offered his services as a nurse to anyone in need, he received a new name: Martin of Charity.

His medical clinic in the Dominican monastery where he lived as a lay brother was always full of sick people due to the myriad and often miraculous healings that took place there. But Brother Martin would explain with a smile, "I merely take care of you, while it is God who heals you." Thus the fame of the holy lay friar spread, and the ranks of the poor and sick increased.

Particularly tormenting his heart, however, was the situation of orphans, which he knew all too well. Left to themselves, they were reduced to wandering the streets as beggars with no hope of education or even redemption. Therefore, he founded an institute for them — *El Asilo de Santa Cruz* — the first boarding school of its kind in the New World. He opened its doors to homeless children who came by the dozens, and he provided them not only with nourishment but also with salaried workers and educators. For girls, he offered an appropriate dowry for when they arrived at the age of marriage.

In all this, a kind of miraculous "social healing" took place. Eventually, Brother Martin came to be respected by the viceroy, the governor, the bishop, and an innumerable host of well-to-do people who supported him with their wealth. Thus part of the wealth plundered by those in power returned to the poor through the holy hands of the "mulatto" friar. In fact, Martin was even proclaimed "patron saint of social justice."

2. St. Katharine Mary Drexel (1858-1955)

She was born Katharine Mary Drexel in Philadelphia to one of the wealthiest families in the state of Pennsylvania in the United States. Yet she chose to dedicate her life and possessions to American Indians after reading a book about the persecutions, injustices, and transgressions committed against them by the government, which were defined by the author even as "true genocide."

She began assessing the problem by visiting several Indian reservations in the American West. She then undertook a similar trip to the South, where she discovered the miserable living conditions of African-Americans. Despite the abolition of slavery, blacks were still working on plantations where they were oppressed and poorly paid. The harsh laws of racial segregation were still in force and blacks had virtually no rights, education, or health care. So Katharine began to spend her sizable fortune on the construction of schools on Indian reservations and in African-American ghettos. However, she realized it was not enough.

Thus, in 1891, with thirteen companions, she founded a new religious congregation approved by Rome with the official name Blessed Sacrament for Indians and Colored People. As part of their vows, members of the congregation promised not to "undertake any work which would lead to the neglect or abandonment of the Indian or Colored races." The reference to the Eucharist was a necessary reminder that "Christ gave himself as food for all people regardless of race or color."

The order began opening boarding schools for children of the pueblos and dormitories for African-American girls. These were followed by missions, churches, schools, boarding houses, and formation houses scattered throughout twenty-one states in the East and West where Native Americans were concentrated and in all southern states where blacks were languishing. In 1925, in the city of New Orleans, the order established the first institution of higher learning in the United States for African-Americans: Xavier University.

Despite being harshly persecuted, the nuns vehemently responded to every self-righteous objection that they would make no distinction between "children of whites," "children of blacks," or "children of savages" (as Native Americans were called then). Instead, they saw only "children of God." In this regard, they said beautifully, "How truly was the Cave of Bethlehem the great educator of the world!"

In sixty years of active service, Katharine dispensed roughly $20 million toward the foundation of 145 Catholic missions, twelve schools for Native Americans, fifty schools for African-Americans and forty-nine convents for five hundred sisters who were completely devoted to their education. At her death, some wondered, "What America and what the Catholic Church might have been in respect to minorities had she not come along." And many also recognized that Katharine Drexel "saved the Church from embarrassment in terms of social justice."

3. *Servant of God Dorothy Day* (1897-1980)

Dorothy Day arrived at doing holy works of mercy in a roundabout way after having lived for many years in a wild search for truth and holiness, which she had never hitherto found. She had been an atheist, anarchist, socialist, objector, and a rebel. Yet in her, it was said, there was also "the way of life of St. Francis of Assisi, the prophetic courage of Catherine of Siena, the dynamism of Teresa of Ávila, the trust in Providence of [Joseph Benedict] Cottolengo, and the spirit of hospitality of St. John of God." But despite all her peculiar experiences, a desire to pray welled up overwhelmingly within her.

She converted at the age of twenty-five when she literally threw herself into the arms of God and the Church. She renounced all other security and spent the rest of her life supporting her Movement in defense of social struggles she considered just. She always reaffirmed that "to see Christ in the other, to love him and take care of him is synonymous with Heaven, because to live in union with God is a foretaste of heavenly joy. Those who live with this awareness within themselves are saints." But she argued with equal vigor that "those who cannot see Christ in the poor are atheists indeed." Her "workers" were often of different ideological opinions, and so she spoke frequently and only of "works of mercy." She didn't know any better term to describe the ideals of the Catholic Worker Movement, which she founded in 1933.

She made only one demand: that every house had at least one room for prayer where anyone could go freely whenever they wanted. The important thing was that visitors could clearly see that there was a praying heart in each house: "We feed the hungry, yes. We try to shelter the homeless and give them clothes, but there is strong faith at work; we pray. If an outsider who comes to visit us doesn't pay attention to our prayings and what that means, then he'll miss the whole point."

Dorothy has been called "the anarchist of God." Yet on her tombstone is depicted a simple basket of loaves and fishes and an inscription reading: "*Deo gratias*" ("Thanks be to God").

4. *Servant of God Brother Ettore Boschini* (1928-2004)

A lay brother in the order of St. Camillus in the northern Italian city of Milan, Ettore Boschini devoted his life to the marginalized:

homeless people, beggars, aging prostitutes, alcoholics, and drug addicts. At first, he would meet with them in the streets and try to offer as much comfort as possible. But he soon realized, however, that this wasn't enough. So he sought to provide stable housing for them by outfitting two large uninhabited warehouses underneath a train station. Some Milanese people referred to the shelter as "Brother Ettore's cathedral."

From then on, he began to walk the streets and alleyways of Milan for nights on end. He would stop by every homeless person dressed in rags and gently invite them to his shelter saying, "Come with me."

And since the number of "guests" who were in need of specialized housing was expanding, Brother Ettore expanded the shelters, giving rise to new centers even in foreign countries. He once went all the way to Colombia [in South America] to establish a house for street children. People there later said of him:

> He was a saint who lived in different eras at the same time. He was an unarmed warrior — like the saints of the past — who made his way among desperate people, even the most dangerous, with a smile and the strength of faith. But he was also a contemporary man of technology who knew how to use a computer and a cellphone.

Another person called him "a mystic as solid as a laborer."

CHAPTER NINE

In Mission of Mercy
Toward Those Far Off

St. Peter Claver / Venerable Marcello Candia

1. *St. Peter Claver* (1581-1654)

While still a young Jesuit student in Palma de Mallorca, Spain, Peter Claver listened to the invitation of the old doorkeeper of his community. He told the young Peter about what was happening in the New World: "The souls of the Indians have infinite value because they, too, have the same cost of the blood of Christ.… Go to the Indies and purchase all those lost souls!"

Thus Peter petitioned his superiors to allow him to go to Cartagena, Colombia, where slave ships with more than a thousand slaves arrived at the city's port each month. Having no recourse to social or political action, Peter nevertheless soon decided to place himself at the service of the poor slaves. He introduced himself to them as "a slave of the black people forever," and he worked to give them the dignity they could never aspire to: that of feeling loved.

Peter immediately set out to give every possible aid to every slave he met and sought to acquire the basic necessities and comforts for them through begging. Then, beginning with those who arrived moribund from exhaustion, he presented an extraordinary catechesis. He utilized large posters that he personally painted in bright colors to recount the life and mercy of Jesus crucified. Next, Peter used other illustrated boards in a similar manner to tell the Gospel, to explain the truths of the Christian faith, and to teach the Commandments. And he was convinced he had truly touched the hearts of the poor black slaves when they repeated the formula verbatim that he had taught them persistently, repeatedly, and weeping with emotion: "Jesus Christ, Son of God, you are my father, my mother, and all my goodness. I love you very much, and I feel extreme pain for having offended you. Lord, I love you very, very, very much."

In time, Peter Claver would learn to speak various dialects and gathered around him numerous catechists. Eventually, he was proclaimed the universal patron of missions to black people.

2. Venerable Marcello Candia (1916-1983)

Marcello Candia was once a wealthy businessman who became a pauper by giving away everything he had — including himself. During his youth and young adulthood, Marcello learned how to combine work with the wise administration of his assets and an even more attentive and active social charity. Later, a series of events led him to befriend several Brazilian missionaries. He then concluded: "It is not enough to occasionally give economic assistance. We must share with the poor their lives, as much as possible. It would be too easy for me to remain over here in my easy and privileged life and say, 'I'll send my leftovers over there.' Instead, I am called to go and live with them."

He moved to Macapà, Brazil, where he founded and ran a hospital "for the poorest of the poor." He also established a comfortable leper hospital in Marituba, in northern Brazil. He spent the last eighteen years of his life in the country where he promulgated "deeds and works" consisting of nursing homes, schools, villages, leprosaria, convents, seminaries, churches, and volunteer centers. He went as far as Belo Horizonte, Brazil, to the *favelas* of Rio de Janeiro, and even to the border with Bolivia.

A friend who sometimes visited him in his missions said of him:

Candia was dynamic, self-confident, and accustomed to being in charge and always speaking. He was also very generous and beneficent, and he had large resources available. But he was also conscientious of having a lot and knowing how to use it.... But every time he went back into the Amazon, he came out transformed. He realized that he needed other people in order to realize all his aspirations. It was a remarkable change: he went from being a man at the center of his world to being a servant to all people.... He truly felt he was at the service of everyone God brought him into contact with.

Candia wrote the following on the walls of his home in Brazil: "One cannot share in heavenly Bread if one cannot share his earthly bread."

CHAPTER TEN

Mercy or Revolution?

St. Albert Chmielowski or Vladimir Lenin?

St. Albert Chmielowski (1845-1916)

Albert's baptismal name was Adam, and he was known as a promising and brilliant painter in Warsaw, Poland, where he was from. His strong Christian faith kept forcing him to seek an answer to the same questions: "What is the purpose of art?" and "What is the fate of the artist?"

He had long been dedicated to the realization of a painting which he called *Ecce Homo* ("Behold the Man"). Yet he was never able to finish it until he realized that he would not be able to create the masterpiece he was dreaming of until he first dedicated himself to the restoration of the image of the suffering Christ in the poor. Today, his completed *Ecce Homo* adorns his gravesite.

He wore a poor tunic and referred to himself as Brother Albert. He started out by taking care of poor people within his own home. He soon felt called to visit the homeless where they were huddled in the Kraków public dormitories — and where aristocrats, such as he, never dared to venture. In fact, as soon as he set foot in the shelter, he was threatened with death. At that moment, however, Chmielowski understood that their want was so excessive that it could not be consoled or relieved, except on one condition: "We must live among them! We cannot leave them." So he sold all his paintings and went to live with the poor.

He took advantage of the warm summer months, when the residents vacated the awful shelters, to restore and embellish them, transforming them into "assistance homes." At that point he became a beggar and sought alms for his homeless people.

When the people saw him seated on his huge cart built purposely for begging alms and going back and forth through the markets, they said: "Behold Adam Chmielowski — the man who was once a famous painter has become father to the poor!" He asked for alms with humility and a sweet smile, and he received the people's donations with tears of gratitude in his eyes. It was impossible to tell who was happier — those who gave or he who received.

He gathered numerous coworkers around him. There were so many, in fact, that he founded a congregation for men and another for women. All who sought to enter had to practice absolute poverty: the first thing they had to do was give away everything they owned to the poor. It was as if another St. Francis of Assisi was living in the streets of Kraków.

Brother Albert explained to his collaborators: "I look at Jesus in his Eucharist. Could his love perhaps provide anything more beautiful? If He is bread, we ourselves become bread and give ourselves." And he said to them tirelessly, "We must become as good as bread."

The story of Brother Albert is not very different from other ones we have recounted thus far. However, it deserves to be considered separately because of the strong relevance he had on his culture. We must not forget, in fact, that Brother Albert worked in Poland during the years just before the Communist Revolution broke out in Russia. Certainly, he, too, must have considered how the intolerable plight of the poor foreshadowed the fire that was about to break out and destroy society. And, in fact, an extraordinary detail within the acts of Brother Albert's canonization process shows that he had the occasion to meet Vladimir Lenin, who was exiled in Kraków at that time. It seems they spoke, asking themselves several questions: "Does the strength of the poor lie in their anger when it is appropriately guided and channeled? Or is their strength in charity, solidarity, and in the rediscovery of Christian radicalism?" The question was, then, mercy or revolution?

Subsequently, a newly ordained priest decided to write a play about the story of Brother Albert. Born just four years after Chmielowski's death, the young Polish priest's name was Karol Wojtyla. Written in 1949 and titled *Our God's Brother* (in Italian, *Fratello del nostro Dio*. Vatican City: LEV, 1982), the future pontiff's play tells the story of Adam Chmielowski's meeting with Lenin, who is referred to as "the Stranger." (In 1997, film director Krzysztof Zanussi made it into a film.)

At first, the dejected "painter of charity" endures the shocking accusation hurled at him by the Stranger: charity serves only to keep the poor in poverty and leaves them "twice humiliated. Twice: once by poverty and another by charity."

"This is not the right way!" the revolutionary insists. "Charity does not strengthen their immense collective anger; instead, it discharges and blunts it. You deceive the people! Your charity only serves to diffuse the strength of the people!" Then the Stranger enters the shelter and pleads to the people in the dormitories: "Do not sit around waiting for charity! Charity will humiliate you! You do not need it! You must understand that absolutely everything belongs to you. Nothing is of grace. Charity is a stretched-out shadow in which a mysterious, incomprehensible, wealthy person attempts to hide his true face. Beware of the apostles of charity! They are your enemies!"

Meanwhile, Adam is seated in a corner whispering slowly but over and over as if his heart were echoing the sentiments of the poor: "Try to put yourself in our place. Try to put yourself in our place …" And, in fact, a voice rises up from the chorus of the poor people who throw the speaker out: "You are far from us, and we are far from you." And another voice insists: "You see, we know only one thing: those who live with us know everything about us. Others know nothing."

In the end, Brother Albert explains to the Stranger his irreparable mistake: "The misery of humanity," he says, "is the largest of all the available goods you speak of. It is bigger than all the goods humanity can obtain with the strength of their anger." Then he adds, gracefully: "I am sure, and I know and believe, that man must obtain all the goods. All of them. Even the biggest. But here at this point wrath deceives; here there is only need of charity."

While such dialogue may appear to be mere artistic imagination devoid of historical fact, the truth is much more profound and complex. In fact, Karol Wojtyla, who had already imitated Brother Albert as a young man, wrote all the words. The future pontiff had found the strength in the example of this poor brother to renounce his artistic passion for the theater in order to "give himself entirely" to the priesthood. After becoming pope, his youthful reflections on "revolution of charity" made while writing about the mission of the painter-brother would become papal teaching. They would be truths proclaimed openly to the world and to all nations where Christians were tempted to entrust the liberation of the poor to violent revolutionaries.

One example of the maturation of St. John Paul II's youthful insight is his encyclical *Dives in Misericordia* (on the mercy of God). And though Brother Albert died on the eve of the Bolshevik Revolution, which may have seemed to lend credence to Lenin's social thought (as it affected world history for decades), in the end — through the actions and teachings of St. John Paul II — the message of Brother Albert would triumph over every Marxist-Leninist utopia. It was not by chance, in fact, that Pope John Paul II chose to canonize Chmielowski on that fateful day of 1989 which marked the end of communism.

CHAPTER ELEVEN

A Strong and Merciful "Father"

Blessed Titus Brandsma

Virtually everyone is familiar with the parable of the merciful father who welcomes back the prodigal son, as it has been told and imitated a thousand times in Christian history. Here, however, we would like to describe an actual historical exemplification of this parable. In the following story, fatherhood is encapsulated in the act of the merciful "regeneration" of a lost soul who converts even as she is responsible for killing the person who prompted her regeneration.

What follows is the powerful story of Father Titus Brandsma (1881-1942), a Dutch Carmelite priest who was deported and killed by the Nazis in the infamous Dachau concentration camp. (Source: Romeral, F. Millán. *Il coraggio della verità. Il Beato Tito Brandsma*. Ancora, 2012.) At 59 years old, Father Brandsma was a professor of philosophy and the history of mysticism at the Catholic University of Nijmegen in the Netherlands, where he also had the title of *Rector Magnificus*.

As early as 1936 — in an era when news was not well disseminated or very reliable — he collaborated on a book entitled *Dutch Voices on the Treatment of Jews in Germany*. He wrote: "What is happening now against the Jews is an act of cowardice. The enemies and adversaries of that people are truly wretched if they believe they must act in such an inhumane way and if they think such action manifests or increases the strength of the German people. This is an illusion of weakness."

German officials responded by classifying him an "evil professor." Yet he was aware of his responsibility as a teacher, and he did not back down. In the academic year of 1938-39, he was already teaching on the "disastrous trends" of National Socialism (Nazism). His course dealt with the following fundamental arguments: the value and dignity of each and every human being whether healthy or sick; the equality and inherent goodness of all races; the indestructible and primary value of natural law over ideology; the presence and guidance of God throughout human history against political messianism; and idolatry of power. And all the while, he was aware that there were (Nazi) party spies present in his audience.

In 1941, the question exploded as to whether or not Catholic newspapers in the Netherlands should publish press releases and advertisements of the Dutch National Socialist Movement as required by a new law. Father Titus — who was then spiritual director to Catholic journalists — wasted no time in circulating the following memorandum: "Publishers and editors should know that they will have to formally reject such communications if they wish to preserve the Catholic identity of their newspapers. And they should do so even if such refusal leads to the newspaper being threatened, fined, or suspended temporarily or even permanently. There is nothing else possible to do. With this, we have reached our limit. Otherwise, they shall no longer be considered Catholic … and they shall not, nor will they be able to rely on Catholic readers and subscribers any longer, and they shall end in disgrace."

A few months later, Professor Brandsma was arrested and deported to the notorious Dachau concentration camp where he was subjected to every manner of humiliation and torture. And when it finally became necessary to admit him to the field hospital, his fate was sealed. We know what happened due to an exceptional eyewitness: the following account comes from the woman herself who killed him and who later converted because she could not rid herself of the memory of Father Titus.

She was a nurse by profession, but she obeyed the inhumane orders of the medical officers out of fear. She said that when Father Titus "was admitted into the infirmary, he was already on the 'dead list.'" She also described how sick experiments were performed on the patients (which she opposed) — including on Father Titus — and how its memory was burned within her. She said that the priest endured the abuse, repeating over and over, "Father, not my will, but may yours be done." She related how all the patients hated her and routinely insulted her with the most disparaging names. (Such hatred was cordially reciprocated.) However, she was struck by the way the elderly priest treated her, instead, with the gentleness and respect of a father. She said, "He once took my hand and said to me, 'What a poor girl you are, I will pray for you.'"

The prisoner gave her his own poor rosary made of copper and wood. However, this only irritated her, and she said she had no need of such an object because she did not know how to pray. Father Titus, however, responded: "You need not say the entire Hail Mary. Say only, 'Pray for us sinners.'"

On that fateful day of July 25, 1942, the ward doctor handed her the syringe filled with carbolic acid to inject into Father Titus' veins. It was a routine procedure which the nurse had already done hundreds of times. Yet the poor woman later recalled "feeling sick for the rest of the day." The injection was administered at 1:50 p.m. and Father Titus died at 2:00 p.m. "I was there when he died," the nurse later testified. "The doctor was sitting next to his bed with a stethoscope for the sake of appearances. When Father Tito's heart stopped beating, he commented, 'This pig is dead.'"

Father Titus always spoke well about his captors and torturers: "They, too, are children of the good God, and perhaps something still remains within them." And God would grant him this final miracle. The camp doctor sarcastically referred to the poisonous syringe as an "injection of grace." And while the nurse injected it into his veins, it was the intercession of Father Titus that truly instilled the grace of God within her. And during the process of canonization, the poor woman explained that the image of that old priest remained forever impressed in her memory. She saw something in his face that she had never before experienced. She said simply: "He had compassion on me." Like Christ.

CHAPTER TWELVE

A Merciful Mother

St. Gianna Beretta Molla

The original biblical meaning of the term "mercy," as many people are aware, refers to the maternal affection a mother has for the child she carries within her womb. And there are certainly countless examples of such unwavering maternal love. But mercy is present in a particular way when the mother herself is asked to love "more" — in a way often misunderstood by others. Such is the case of St. Gianna Beretta Molla (1922-1962): a woman, wife, mother, and passionate doctor.

She wrote in her diary:

> The beauty of our mission: All of us who work in the world work at some level in the service of people. We [doctors], however, work directly with people. The object of our knowledge and work is the human being before us who says to us, "Help me!" and expects from us the fullness of his or her life.... Yet, our mission is not finished when medicine is no longer needed; the soul needs to be brought to God. In fact, Jesus says: "I was sick and you visited me." The priestly mission: As the priest touches Jesus, so we doctors touch Jesus in the body of our patients

— the poor, young, elderly, and children. May Jesus make himself seen among us. May He find many doctors who offer themselves for Him. (Source for this chapter: Molla and Guerriero. *La beata Gianna Beretta Molla nel ricordo del marito.* Cinisello Balsamo: San Paolo, 1995)

And if Gianna was able to "touch Jesus" while taking care of her patients and giving herself for them, it was because this same "touch" was continuously present in her family. While courting her future husband, Pietro, she wrote the following words — intense in terms of vocation and prophetic in holiness:

> Pietro, if I could only tell you everything I feel for you! But I'm not able to. Fill in the words yourself. The Lord himself loved me. You are the man I desired to meet, but I do not deny that I sometimes ask myself if I will be worthy of him. Yes, worthy of you, Pietro, because I feel like I am nothing and capable of nothing. In fact, while I greatly desire to make you happy, I fear I won't be able to. And so I pray thus to the Lord: "Lord, you who know my feelings and my good will, find a solution and help me to become a wife and a mother as you wish and as I think Pietro desires." Is that good, Pietro?

As their marriage approached, she wrote to him again saying:

> With the help and blessing of God, we shall do everything so that our new family may be a little Cenacle [Last Supper], where Jesus reigns over all our affections, desires, and actions. My Pietro, only a few days remain [before our marriage] and I feel so moved to draw near and receive the sacrament of Love. We shall become collaborators of God in His creation, and, thus, we can give Him children who love Him and serve Him.

Her husband later recalled the beauty of their marriage, enriched by three children:

> You were always busy in the house: I can't remember you remaining idle even once.… Despite the commitments of our family, you strove to continue your mission as a doctor in Mesero, especially due to the affection and love that tied you to your young mothers, elderly patients, and chronically ill.… Your intentions and actions were always in full compliance with your faith, with your spirit … with the charity of your youth, with full trust in Providence, and with your spirit of humility. In all circumstances, you always called on and entrusted yourself to the will of the Lord. I remember that you always put aside time every day for prayer and meditation, conversation with God, and gratitude for the gift of our wonderful children. And you were so happy.

Before talking about Gianna's mysterious encounter with maternal merciful love, we would first like to emphasize the fact that all Christians are called to holiness — that is, called to allow God's mercy to permeate their days and their entire lives in all aspects. And we speak of "mercy" for the fact that it is always present whenever human love exceeds the measures as dictated by the norm, habits, conveniences, and merit, to the point that one always moves immersed in the ocean of merciful love of God. Without considering this "divine immersion," it is impossible to correctly understand the experience of this mother who gave her own life to guarantee the life of the child she was carrying in her womb.

Her husband thoroughly explained the meaning of the gift his wife gave to all humanity:

> Gianna did what she did not merely "to get to heaven."
> What she did, she did as a mother.… To understand her

decision, we cannot forget, first of all, her deep conviction — as a mother and as a doctor — that the creature
she was carrying within her was a complete creature
with the same rights as her other children, even if she
[our unborn daughter] had only been conceived for just
about two months. She was still a gift from God who
deserved sacred respect. Neither can one forget the great
love Gianna had for her other children: she loved them
more than she loved herself. And we mustn't forget her
trust in Providence. She was convinced, in fact, as a wife
and as a mother, that she was extremely *necessary* to me
and to our children. However, she knew that at that very
moment she was *indispensable* to the little creature who
was growing inside her.

Thus, fully aware that her final pregnancy could cost Gianna
her life due to uterine cancer, she chose — in the words of Blessed
Paul VI — "conscious immolation."

She told her husband and doctors resolutely, "Save the child, not
me." To better understand the value of her "choice," let's listen to her
husband's reflection, who shared, in the same faith, the decision of
his wife, but who was not able to think about it or even talk about
it. He later testified:

Her request to "save the pregnancy" kept running over
and over in my mind. But I didn't dare go any further
with the thought. Nor did I dare talk about it with my
wife. At some point later she said, "Pietro, you have
always been so loving with me, and I need you to be
even more so during this period, because these past few
months have been harsh for me." She always seemed to
me to be calm. She continued to have her usual amount
of affection for our children and for her patients. Then
one day I realized that she was cleaning up the house

with particular attention. She was rearranging the
drawers and armoires ... as if she were about to go away
on a long journey.

Certainly, Gianna had her moments of distress and anxiety.
On her deathbed, she confessed to her sister, "If you only knew
how much someone suffers when they leave their children who are
so young ..."

What, then, could have driven her to make that choice? Most
certainly it was her clear conscience, without any doubts, of living
in obedience to the God who commands, "Thou shalt not kill." As
a doctor, she had once said to a girl who asked her to perform an
abortion, "You don't mess around with children."

Yet, this obedience sprang from another conviction that was
also obvious to her: one cannot take care of three children at the
expense of another.

And here, we finally arrive in our journey at the decisive word
— an ancient word that offers the only light when life is too dark
and incomprehensible: God's *Providence*. When there is no sense
of divine Providence, people become restless and live by their own
will, to the point of believing that killing will improve their own
life and the lives of others. On the other hand, when there is a
humble, simple, and ancient faith in Providence, as conveyed by the
filial and paternal face of Christ, then human reason will be able to
perceive its evidence — a "reasoned reaction" as her husband coura-
geously wrote. And the evidence demonstrated that while Gianna
was "necessary" for the other three children, she was "indispensable" for the child she was carrying in her womb. Without her,
God could "provide for" the other children. Yet not even God could
"provide" for the child she was carrying in her womb if Gianna
had refused her. For this reason, as the months passed, suffering
increased within her, but so did tenderness toward the little girl
growing inside her.

Let us now return to the painful story of Gianna's husband.

A month and a half before the birth of our child, something happened that upset me. I had to leave to go to the factory and I had already put my coat on. Gianna — I can still see her — was leaning on the furniture in the foyer of our house. She moved close to me. She did not say to me, "Let's sit down," "Wait a moment," or "Let's talk." Nothing like that. Instead, she moved close to me as when someone is about to say something difficult and heavy that they've reflected on and do not want to go back. "Peter," she told me, "I beg you … if a choice has to be made between me and the baby, make the decision for the child, not for me. I ask this of you."

Shortly before delivery, she said something similar in a conversation with a friend. "I'm going to the hospital now," she said, "but I'm not sure if I'll ever come home. My pregnancy has been so difficult. I fear they're going to have to save one or the other; I want my baby to live." But her friend responded, "But you have three other children, you should be concerned instead about your own life." But Gianna said, "No, no … I want my baby to live." She met another friend while at the hairdresser's to whom she said: "Please pray, pray! I have studied and prayed so much for my new creation during this difficult pregnancy. Pray for me so that I am ready to do the will of God."

And God willed her passion to begin precisely on Good Friday in 1962. A sister in the hospital recounted: "I met her as she climbed the steps to be admitted to the maternity ward. She said to me, 'Sister, here I am, I am here to die.' But she had a good and serene disposition. She added: 'The important thing is that all goes well for the baby; as for me, I do not matter.'"

The terrible labor lasted the entire night, and the birth took place at 11a.m. on Holy Saturday morning. When she awoke from the anesthesia, they brought Gianna her newborn baby girl. Her husband later said: "She gazed at her silently for a very long time.

Gianna held her close with indescribable tenderness. She caressed her gently without saying a word."

Gianna died one week later from septic peritonitis. There was nothing that could have been done to save her. Her husband had the back wall of the mortuary where her body was initially laid covered with a golden mosaic. In it, Gianna is depicted offering her child to Our Lady of Lourdes with an inscription, written in Latin, taken from the Book of Revelation: *Esto fidelis usque ad mortem* ("Be faithful unto death" [Rv 2:10]).

Gianna Beretta Molla's death was precisely "merciful fidelity," which, in the beautiful words of the prophet Isaiah, can be summarized thus: she was a mother who preferred to "forget herself" rather than forget — even for an instant — "the child of her womb" whom only she could save (see Is 49:15).

CHAPTER THIRTEEN

A Most Merciful Spouse

Blessed Elizabeth Canori Mora

Today, there is a lot of talk about how so many hurt spouses and wounded families are in need of mercy — overwhelmed as they are by so many problems and conflicts they can no longer endure. But perhaps we should first speak of mercy in terms of how spouses in crisis could humbly practice it the moment the family begins to fall apart. Sometimes the family can be saved when mercy is practiced patiently by even just one member who is capable of hoping and loving with hope.

Such was the case of Elizabeth Canori Mora (1774-1825) whom Pope John Paul II beatified together with Gianna Beretta Molla in 1994, the Year of the Family, referring to them both as "women of heroic love." (Source: Redi, Paolo. *Elisabetta Canori Mora. Un amore fedele tra le mura di casa*. Roma: Città Nuova, 1994.)

The marriage between Elizabeth, from a noble Roman family, and Cristoforo Mora, a young, wealthy attorney, seemed like a fairy tale come true — at least in the beginning. It was said that Cristoforo was thunderstruck by Elizabeth's beauty. In fact, he swore he would never, ever seek any other woman if she would only consent to marry him. Yet he worried at the thought that her beauty might be tarnished, and so he did not want his wife to tire herself or do any work that might wear her down. Neither would he allow her to engage in sewing or embroidery, so that her fingers would not become rough. Yet his jealousy became still more obsessive, and he soon even forbade his wife from having any contact even with her own relatives.

But after a few months, his obsessive jealousy was followed by icy coldness, and he became increasingly distracted and absent. He began to leave the house early in the morning and come home late at night. There was talk around town that he had gotten involved with a woman of low status who was bleeding him financially. The young lawyer never felt like he had enough money, and his gambling losses increased to the point of bankruptcy. To pay for her husband's increasing debts Elizabeth sold all her jewelry. Yet even her money seemed to disappear in a bottomless pit. Unable to keep up the lifestyle they were accustomed to, the two were forced to move into a small apartment next to the home of her in-laws. By now, Elizabeth was completely neglected by her husband, and she was forced to support herself and provide for the children by the work of her hands. And she felt more and more alone. Furthermore, she was gripped by severe stomach pains. But this is where her wonderful mystical journey began.

At this point, we might be tempted to consider such a "mystical journey" in facile — even trite — terms. Here it seems that we have a woman — betrayed by her husband, deprived of affection, seriously ill, with no means of raising her children — who apparently channels her problems into an intense but artificial, spiritual, and emotional world she had created for herself.

For believers, however, there is a simpler, more enlightening explanation. We know that Christian marriage — with all its accompanying gifts and graces — is a sacrament. It is both a means to and a sign of a far greater and much more profound reality. And this reality indicated therein is the Love of Jesus who is both Lover and Beloved and who embraces both spouses. But if one of the two is absent, who is to say that he cannot decide to reveal this reality of the "sacred marriage" such as when an actor in the background enters the forestage?

This is what happened to Elizabeth: as a sign, she had sacramentally received her husband, who later renounced her and betrayed her. Then the true Bridegroom, the only One, decided to reclaim his rightful place. And he decided to do so in this case mystically "with the senses" — that is, by revealing his presence extraordinarily. But take note: certain mystical experiences of the saints are indeed unique and extraordinary. However, as the *Catechism of the Catholic Church* says, God grants "special graces or extraordinary signs of this mystical life ... only to some for the sake of manifesting the gratuitous gift given to all" (2014). And the gift is, namely, the ordinary grace granted in all sacramental marriages. In fact, sooner or later every Christian spouse must — partly in suffering, partly in joy — understand the distance that exists, in love, between the creature and the Creator.

The mystical life of Elizabeth was, as such, rich in prayers, visions, and delightful amorous raptures. Her days were spent in total union with the Lord beginning with Mass early in the morning when she received daily Communion. She devoted the rest of her day to caring for her girls, domestic work, and prayer. Cristoforo was hardly ever around. When he did show up late at night, Elizabeth was always there, wide awake, waiting for him. She made a decision never to argue with him and to only offer kind words and encouragement to change his life. In her free time, she devoted herself to traditional works of mercy: with the permission of her mother-in-law, the only one who really understood her and supported her, she gathered leftovers from the kitchen and went to visit the sick in the hospitals, taking on even the most humble and repugnant tasks.

In an effort to ensure the family inheritance for themselves alone, Cristoforo's sisters denounced him to the authorities for immoral behavior. He ran the risk of imprisonment, which he managed to avoid only by promising to repent. Yet when he returned to his family, he was even more infuriated. His rage was so intense that he was even tempted to kill his wife. He later recounted that each time he felt tempted to do so, he felt a power greater than himself block his arm. Everyone counseled Elizabeth to leave the house and seek shelter elsewhere, but she refused. Not even his relatives could understand how she could stay alone at night with a man who threatened to kill her.

Elizabeth questioned her Lord Jesus regarding this and received the following answer: "that I was not to abandon these three souls — namely, my two daughters and husband — as he wanted to save them through me." Given the risk she was running, even her confessor suggested she separate from her husband. Instead, she replied, "I place the salvation of these three souls before my spiritual profit." She reassured him by telling him that she fell asleep praying like a child: "My spirit was resting gently in the arms of the Lord and a beam of light surrounded me and made my rest sure."

What is more striking in this story is not the mention of the beam of light that protected her, but the fact that these two souls were in such close marital contact: one was lost in the throes of darkness and vice, while the other was immersed in the protective light of spousal friendship with Christ. And we're not talking about two stories that opposed and annulled one another, but instead of a mysterious connection.

Thus Elizabeth continued on in relative serenity, alternating between work, prayer, and taking care of her girls. Her life was enveloped with moments of grace in which Jesus offered her symbolic visions of the most sublime truths of the Faith. And when her daughters got a little older and Elizabeth began to worry about aspects of their behavior and how she would provide for them, Jesus said to her: "Do not fear, from now on I will come in person and act as father and master of the household. From now on, you will have not only what is necessary for yourself and your family, but what is overabundant." So, through an extraordinary set of circumstances, her household — which could not become a "domestic church" due to the absence of a husband who was a spendthrift and a woman-izer — became an "authentic church" due to the intervention of the heavenly Bridegroom who personally substituted her deficient spouse. And the miracles were innumerable.

Meanwhile, Elizabeth entered the Third Order of the Most Holy Trinity — an order born in antiquity to liberate enslaved Christians — and her spirituality became more and more focused on serving the poorest and most destitute. She was concerned for the salvation of all people, and she therefore prayed increasingly and insistently for the salvation of her husband who continued to live with his mistress.

Her daughters were exasperated, and as they got older, they wished for divine punishment to come down on the mistress, the woman who had taken their father from them. Elizabeth, however, intervened "with strength and energy," explaining to the girls that she, on the other hand, "always prayed to the Lord, telling him that she desired for the woman — who had confounded her husband and caused so much damage — to be near her in heaven." She had a peculiar wish for her husband, as well, telling him, "You, too, will have your Christmas Eve." It was as if she believed that the poor man's mistake was simply that he had not yet experienced the tenderness of the Incarnation.

She had predicted the exact day of her own death for more than a year. Indeed, God gave her a moment by moment foretaste of it in a vision, which she later recounted: "It seemed as if I passed away in the arms of Jesus and Mary while enjoying a paradise of happi-ness." When the fateful day arrived, she said to her daughters, "I am leaving you now to go to your Father, Jesus of Nazareth." Then she urged them to always be respectful of their father and to help him always.

She died on the expected date just after her fiftieth birthday at around 2:00 a.m. in the morning. When Cristoforo came home two hours later, he could not believe that Elizabeth had died. He stood there leaning against the wall stupefied and sobbing. From that day on, he was not the same man. He never said anything to anyone, but just a short time prior to Elizabeth's death, his mistress had died in his arms.

He was now a changed man. He finally began showing interest in things he had hitherto despised, and he no longer cared about fine things or fancy clothing. Instead, he spent long hours in church sobbing and passing an old hat back and forth between his hands. It seemed he was praying with his hat over his face. The fact is that he had pasted a picture of Elizabeth inside the underside of the hat that he kept looking at, and crying. He said that "he had made her holy by his mistreatments."

After nine years had passed since Elizabeth's death, news of an unexpected event spread through Rome: a certain Father Antonio celebrated his first Mass in the (Franciscan) Order of Friars Minor Conventual. The man had been ordained exceptionally at the ripe old age of sixty-one after completing his theology studies. Antonio was the religious name he took in the friary, while in the world he had been known as "the attorney, Cristoforo Mora." According to Elizabeth's promise, he finally received "his Christmas Eve." And after eleven years of remorse, prayer, and penance spent in the friary, he, too, would die reputed to be a saint.

Now, to summarize the teaching conveyed in the story: Mercy, which the family is in need of, is first of all understanding that *in a Christian marriage everything is a sacrament*: the love the couple is able to express with one another is the beautiful part of the sacrament (of the "sacred sign"); the love that a spouse will not or cannot give (with sufferings that follow) must become the virginal part of the sacrament (of the "sacred sign") — the part that defers directly to Christ and directly invokes his presence. If even just one spouse is aware of this, life is filled with mercy and can be filled with miracles.

CHAPTER FOURTEEN

A Merciful Daughter

Blessed Laura Vicuña

There is a singular type of mercy that can be exercised toward adults only by "the little saints": mercy toward their own parents! Little Laura Vicuña (1891-1904), a saint of only twelve years of age, is a special example. (Source for this chapter: D'Attilia, Miela Fagiolo. *Laurita delle Ande*. Milano: Paoline, 2004.)

Laura was originally from Santiago, Chile; however, due to political persecution, her family was forced to flee to near the border with Argentina. When her father died prematurely, her mother, Mercedes, found herself in a hostile land with no means of supporting herself or her family.

There she met a wealthy landowner named Don Manuel Mora. Known for his violent and quarrelsome temper, he was also a gambler and proud of his horses and women, which he flaunted in front of his friends. They called him *el gaucho malo* ("the bad cowboy"), as he treated his herdsmen and women alike as slaves. Before driving off his last mistress, he first branded her with a red-hot iron used on farm animals as he shouted, "So everyone will know you are mine!" And now he had his eyes on Doña Mercedes who was still young and certainly more elegant than the women he was used to keeping around.

He offered her hospitality in his *estancia* ("residence") and the poor thing accepted. In part, she wanted to ensure housing and an education for her girls; in part, she was smitten by the adventurer's perverse charm. It was understood that Don Manuel would put the two girls, still very young, in a nearby boarding school run by the Salesian sisters, for which he gladly agreed to make the annual payment of thirty pesos. The amount was not a problem for him at all, since he often left that much on gambling tables — plus, he wanted to keep the woman.

In school, Laura was good and studious, and she demonstrated that she had "a strong and sweet character." She knew how to be quiet when necessary, to willfully obey, to be accessible and generous to her companions, and to be quick to forgive.

However, as she grew interiorly, she was pained when she came to understand her poor mother's situation. When the nuns spoke to the children about the beauty of Christian marriage, Laura's mind and heart were opened as she realized how her mother had fallen into ruin and lost herself in an attempt to guarantee worldly comforts for her daughters. She suddenly understood where all the material goods came from: the money that supported her education; the many gifts her mother brought her, including the perfumes and bath items Laura enjoyed giving to her friends; and the elegant silk mantillas her mother flaunted when she arrived at the school. The pain was so great that Laura actually fainted in class.

For her first summer vacation, which began in Argentina on Jan. 1, Laura had to return to the farm. She became even more distressed at the situation as she realized just how foreign that large and wealthy mansion was. Honestly, it frightened her. She realized that prayer was not welcome there when her mother urged the girls not to let Mora see them pray. Don Manuel himself shouted that he "did not want little saints" in his house! She also understood why her mother would no longer pray with her children: she was ashamed at being the mistress of an adventurer.

When Laura was finally able to go back to her poor boarding

school — her "paradise" — the nuns realized she was suffering from an inner pain that nothing and no one could heal. But she also had a goal that she focused on with all her innocent hope: the Eucharist. And her hope was so intense that the sisters allowed her to move up the day of her first Communion even though she was only ten years old. They later recounted: "When the little girl received the news that she had so desired, a darkness came over her face and she wept. 'Are you crying, Laura?' the headmistress affectionately asked her... 'Are you not happy?' 'Oh, yes, I am happy,' stammered the little girl as she wiped away the tears that streamed down her cheeks, 'but I am thinking of my mother. My poor mother!'"

Laura noticed that Doña Mercedes had not been receiving the sacraments for some time. She foresaw the further pain that would occur on that great day when her mother could not receive Communion with her! And when the little girl met Jesus for the first time in the Eucharist, her mother stood apart suffering, with her head held low and a strange intensity in her eyes and heart. From that day on, as a simple, good, and docile student, Laura sought only holiness. She seemed to understand that she would encounter more decisive trials in the future.

At the end of 1901, it was time for vacation again, which, according to custom, had to be spent with the family. For young Laura, this was the "the terrible holiday." Doña Mercedes' situation had now become even more difficult: Don Manuel not only had no intention of marrying her, he often mistreated her to remind her that she was just a servant. Yet there were also rumors that he was paying for her daughters' tuition simply to groom a new and younger lover for himself: Laura was growing up and was now beautiful. Even though she was not quite eleven years old, the master did things in a hurry and was impatient. He began to look for any excuse to be alone with the girl.

The time came for the great feast of the shearing of the flocks and the branding of the new animals. Don Manuel expected a dance with Laura, and he counted on her naivety and his skills as a seducer. However, she refused him. And when she did so again several more times throughout the evening, Mora became irritated and demanded that Doña Mercedes oblige her daughter to acquiesce. When he still did not get what he wanted, he ordered Laura's mother to be tied to a post — where he usually attached his mare — and whipped her. Laura's heart was crushed as she saw the extent to which her mother was enslaved.

Then little Laura felt herself violently snatched up and thrown out in the freezing cold of the Andean night. She was forced to spend the night in the dog shelter while her soul was filled with horror. She soon returned to her boarding school poor, since the master now refused to pay for her schooling.

At this point, with that compelling mindset as sometimes only children possess and inasmuch as only God understands, Laura made the decision to literally "give" her life. It took place in April 1902, a few months after the terrible night just recounted.

Laura listened carefully as the priest read the words of Jesus in the parable of the Good Shepherd at church: "The good shepherd lays down his life for the sheep" (Jn 10:11). Certainly, she did not believe she was the merciful Shepherd, or that her mother belonged to her as her lost sheep. Yet she arrived at the logical conclusion all the same: she would give her life for her mother.

She ran to her confessor and asked permission to be able to offer her life to the Sacred Heart for her mother. When she received permission, she fell before the tabernacle and made her offering. She lived peacefully heedful of offering Jesus and Mary all the tenderness she had: loving attention to the other children she assisted in order to support herself and humble obedience to the teachers.

It was clear that the little girl had an authentic interior mystical life. During the canonical process, the headmistress of the school recalled Laura's "innocent expressions": "I think God himself will preserve within me the memory of his Divine Presence, because no matter what I do and wherever I am, I feel that he follows me like a Father helping me and comforting me." Neither does the following expression, as reported by her confessor, seem like something a ten-year-old girl would say: "Whether praying or working, for me it is the same thing. It is the same thing to work or play, pray or sleep. By doing what they command me to do, I do what God wants me to do, and this is what I want to do. This is my best prayer."

On May 24, 1903 — the feast of the Crowning of Our Lady, Help of Christians — the children were involved in the recreation of a beautiful living painting. Laura read a poem that touched all those present and was then placed very close to the statue of the Madonna. Her mother attended the sacred performance. As Laura descended from the stage, she confided to her teacher: "While my head was resting on the hand of my heavenly Mother, I renewed the offering of my life in an even more fervent way. I did so while watching my poor mother who was in front of me. I will be heard, you will see; my heart tells me so."

On July 16, 1903, during a particularly cold and rainy winter, a terrible flood devastated the entire school, and the girls had to be brought to safety on a makeshift boat. Laura's health had already been declining for a long time, but she came out of that wretched ordeal worse with a chest pain that grew ever stronger. Her condition deteriorated rapidly, but she astonished everyone by her serenity. When people asked her how she felt, she invariably replied, "I'm a little better, thank you!" But her favorite ejaculatory prayer was always the same: "Virgin of Carmel, take me to heaven." It seemed she was looking forward to the fulfillment of a promise.

Given her worrying state of health, she had to be brought back to the farm where Don Manuel Mora greeted her coldly and with some sarcasm. After a few months, Laura's health worsened so much that Doña Mercedes decided to take her away from the wretched place. She rented a poor hut made of straw and mud consisting of just two rooms. However, it was only a short distance from her beloved school, so Laura could resume going to class, though sporadically, and finish the year and reconnect with her dear friends.

Mora initially allowed her to do so. But in January 1904, as the summer holidays began, a storm was brewing.

Don Manuel Mora was furious when he showed up at the miserable hovel to drag "his women" away with the pretense of spending the night there. Laura got up from her bed feverishly and shivering in her night camisole: "If he stays, I'm going back to the boarding school," she said intrepidly. And she began to walk off with difficulty. Then the haughtiness of the "gentleman" burst forth as he pounced on the poor defenseless girl, dragged her by the hair and laid into her with insults and violent blows. Only the intervention of the local people managed to free her from his clutches. For Laura, this was the coup de grâce, and everyone sensed that the end was now just a matter of days.

On Jan. 22, she received extreme unction. Then she asked to speak secretly with her confessor for the last time. She needed to request one final special permission. And while she was in the presence of the priest, the little girl decided to reveal her painful secret to her mother: "Mother," she said, "I am dying. I personally asked Jesus for this…. For almost two years, I have offered my life for you for your conversion, so that you might return to him. Will you not give me the joy of seeing you repent before I die?" Meanwhile, her mother was weeping as she knelt at her child's bedside. The revelation struck her at the core of her soul, even if she had already suspected Laura's secret for some time. She was only able to tell her daughter: "I swear to you that I will do what you ask of me…. I am repentant, and God is the witness of my promise." She kept her promise. Indeed, she resisted all Mora's pressures and persecutions for years, and over time she was able to make a decent living for herself.

Laura knew she had fulfilled her mission. On the evening of Jan. 22, 1904, at the sound of the Angelus, she died while kissing her crucifix over and over and saying: "Thank you Jesus, thank you Mary! Now I can die happy." Her companions and all the townspeople rushed to her. And they all said, "A little saint has died!" At the funeral, they saw that Laura's mother approached the sacraments, penitent and trembling. They understood. And those who knew all the tribulations the little girl had been through called upon "Laura, virgin and martyr," while her mother, recalling what her daughter had suffered, nodded through her tears: "Yes, virgin. And martyr for me."

CHAPTER FIFTEEN

Mary, Mother of Mercy

In his wonderful encyclical *Dives in Misericordia* (on the mercy of God), Pope St. John Paul II referred to mercy as "the most stupendous attribute of the Creator and of the Redeemer" (13). No one on earth ever experienced this so radically and intensely as did Mary Most Holy.

When the term "maternal" was used in the Old Testament, it always referred to the visceral tenderness that God had for his creatures. But the Old Testament would never have dared say that a person could "have mercy on God." The reversal occurred, however, with the Incarnation when the Mercy of God toward humanity was manifested in the fact that he allowed a human creature to be his Mother who was, in turn, connected to him viscerally in the physical sense and "mercifully" in the proper sense.

But this would not have been possible had God not always already been, in himself, also "Son." God could not have received this maternal mercy in this world if from all eternity the Divine Person of the Son had not existed in heaven. Thus in the Christmas icon of the Mother — who could unthinkably embrace within her arms the divine Son who has now become the son of man — the "mystery hidden for ages" was revealed: the Father, rich in mercy, sent his own Son into creation, which was made through him and in him. As Pope Francis wrote in *Misericordiae Vultus* (the papal bull proclaiming the Jubiliee Year of Mercy): "Chosen to be the Mother of the Son of God, Mary, from the outset, was prepared by the love of God to be the Ark of the Covenant between God and man. She treasured divine mercy in her heart in perfect harmony with her Son Jesus" (24).

To call Mary, therefore, Mother of Mercy means precisely that she knows like no one else, humanly and viscerally, the mystery of the "sonship of God" and the "viscerals of the Father." Such a mystery also contains the promise, for us, to make us all "sons and daughters in the Son." At Christmas, therefore, Mary embraced all of God's Mercy within her arms, even if such mercy would be fully revealed only in the Paschal Mystery. Here we recall the beautiful meditation of John Paul II in *Dives in Misericordia*:

> Mary is also the one who obtained mercy in a particular and exceptional way, as no other person has. At the same time, still in an exceptional way, she made possible with the sacrifice of her heart her own sharing in revealing God's mercy. This sacrifice is intimately linked with the cross of her Son, at the foot of which she was to stand on Calvary. Her sacrifice is a unique sharing in the revelation of mercy, that is, a sharing in the absolute fidelity of God to His own love ... that was definitively fulfilled through the cross. No one has experienced, to the same degree as the Mother of the crucified One, the mystery of the cross, the overwhelming encounter of divine transcendent justice with love: that "kiss" given by mercy to justice. No one has received into his heart, as much as Mary did, that mystery, that truly divine dimension of the redemption effected on Calvary by means of the death of the Son, together with the sacrifice of her maternal heart, together with her definitive "fiat." (9)

But how were the two *fiat*s, that of Christmas and that of Easter — the two experiences of mercy — linked within her? Let us contemplate her on Calvary, standing upright at the foot of the cross where they nailed her Son. The disciples had fled, and the only people who remained with her were a few faithful women in love with Jesus and John, his beloved disciple. Certainly, Mary, too, was enveloped in the same darkness that obscured the world: the horrendous torture of her Son had wounded her heart, while her soul was wounded by the inexplicable silence of heaven. She knew the mystery of Jesus' conception; she knew that he had the right to call God his Father; she knew that he had been promised a kingdom without end. But there, on the cross, the Son appeared to pray in vain. Jesus said: "My God, my God, why have you forsaken me?" (Mt 27:46) and Mary knew that he was reciting one of the Psalms (see 22:2). She could have even repeated his words with him, but she trembled at the thought of the verses that followed: "Yet you are he who took me from the womb; / you kept me safe upon my mother's breast. / Upon you was I cast from my birth, / and since my mother bore me you have been my God. / Be not far from me, / for trouble is near / and there is none to help" (Ps 22:9-11).

Mary knew the extent to which all those words were true — each one, literally true! She was there to witness to him with the miracle of her own perpetual virginity. She was the Mother who had offered her womb to God. But God, the Father, was now silent. Only a moment before shouting, "It is finished" (Jn 19:30) and giving himself over to the Father with his last thrust of sonship, Jesus himself revealed the mystery to her: from heaven the Father gave the Son for the salvation of all, he handed him over out of love to the hands of sinners. And the Son not only freely consented, but he wanted his Mother on earth to also agree to that sweet and terrible exchange.

But there was more. Mary then understood that she herself took part in that exchange: her Immaculate Conception and the grace that always filled her were fruit of the blood shed by the Son. And, for the first time, she felt with her entire being that she was truly the daughter of her Son, made by him and redeemed by him. "When Jesus saw his mother, and the disciple whom he loved standing near, he said to his mother, 'Woman, behold, your son!' Then he said to the disciple, 'Behold, your mother!'" (Jn 19:26-27). And from that moment on, Mary accepted with the passion of affection and of new birth that she would be Mother to her son, John, and to all the believers he represented. As the *Catechism of the Catholic Church* says, "at the foot of the cross ... Mary is heard as the Woman, the new Eve, the true 'Mother of all the living'" (2618). And from that time onward, the Church understood it had a Mother, and Mary knew she had innumerable children who would always invoke her: "Hail, Mother of Mercy, our life, our sweetness, and our hope."

BIBLIOGRAPHY

The bibliographical and spiritual profiles of the saints cited in this volume can be read in their entirety in the series (in Italian), *"Ritratti di Santi"* ("Portrait of Saints"), published by Father Antonio Maria Sicari through Jaca Book, publisher in Milan, Italy:

A.M. Sicari. *Il primo libro dei Ritratti di Santi* (1988 / 2009-8th edition): (*The first book of Portrait of Saints*):
- St. Camillus de Lellis
- The Holy Curé of Ars
- St. John Bosco
- St. Joseph Benedict Cottolengo

Sicari. *Nuovi Ritratti di Santi* (1988 / 2009-9th edition): (*New Portrait of Saints*):
- St. Vincent de Paul
- St. Thérèse of Lisieux

Sicari. *Il terzo libro dei Ritratti di Santi*: (1993 / 2003-3rd edition): (*The third book of Portrait of Saints*):
- St. John of God
- St. Leopold Mandic
- St. Gianna Beretta Molla

Sicari. *Il quarto libro dei Ritratti di Santi* (1994 / 2003-3rd edition): (*The fourth book of Portrait of Saints*):
- Blessed Damien de Veuster

Sicari. *Il quinto libro dei Ritratti di Santi* (1996 / 2002-2nd edition): (*The fifth book of Portrait of Saints*):
- Blessed Titus Brandsma

Sicari. *Santi del nostro tempo* (1999): (*Saints of our time*):
- Venerable Marcello Candia
- Mother Teresa of Calcutta

Sicari. *Il sesto libro dei Ritratti di Santi* (2000 / 2009-6th edition): (*The sixth book of Portrait of Saints*):
- St. Faustina Kowalska

Sicari. *Il settimo libro dei Ritratti di Santi* (2002): (*The seventh book of Portrait of Saints*):
- Elisabeth Canori Mora
- St. Jerome Emiliani
- St. Peter Claver

Sicari. *Il nono libro dei Ritratti di Santi* (2006): (*The ninth book of Portrait of Saints*):
- St. Elizabeth of Hungary
- Blessed Laura Vicuña
- Blessed Vladimir Ghika
- Servant of God Dorothy Day

Sicari. *Il decimo libro dei Ritratti di Santi* (2007): (*The tenth book of Portrait of Saints*):
- St. Albert Chmielowski
- St. John Paul II

Sicari. *L'undicesimo libro dei Ritratti di Santi* (2009): (*The eleventh book of Portrait of Saints*):
- Servant of God Friedrich Joseph Haass

Sicari. *Il dodicesimo libro dei Ritratti di Santi* (2011): (*The twelfth book of Portrait of Saints*):
- St. Martin de Porres

Sicari. *Il tredicesimo libro dei Ritratti di Santi* (2013): (*The thirteenth book of Portrait of Saints*):
- St. Katharine Mary Drexel
- Servant of God Brother Ettore Boschini